THE ANCIENT WORLD

FROM THE ICE AGE TO THE FALL OF ROME

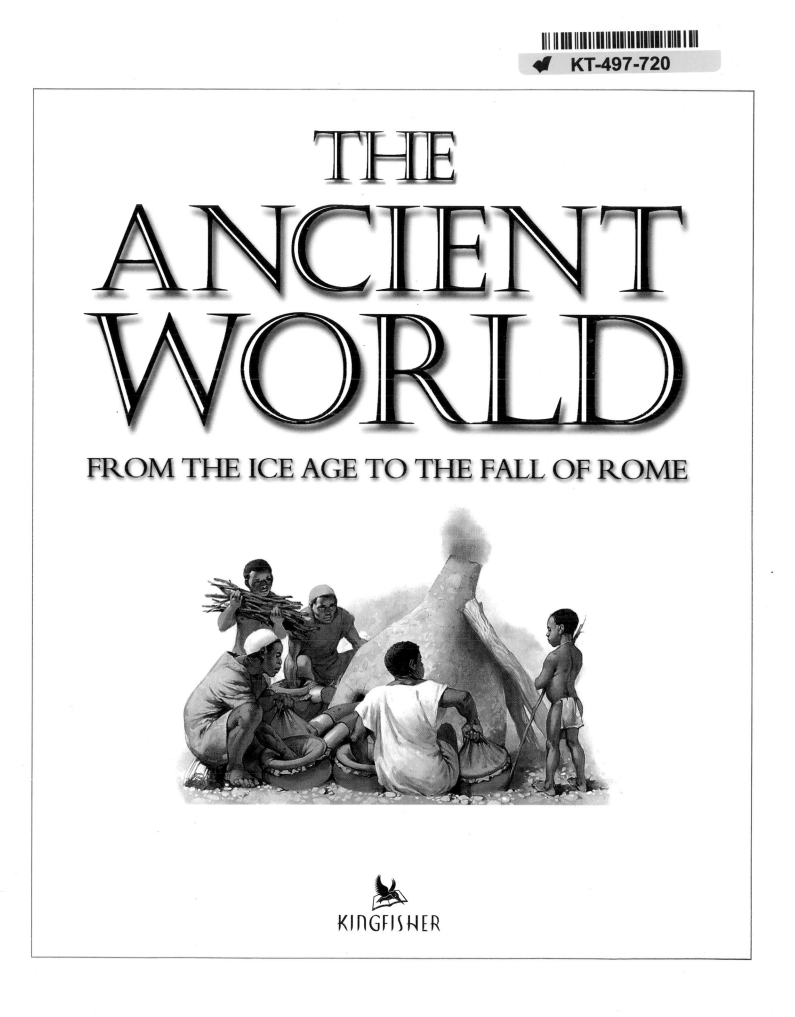

KINGFISHER

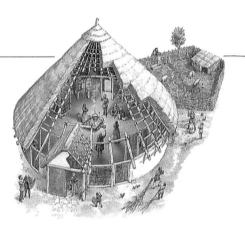

KINGFISHER

Kingfisher Publications Plc
New Penderel House, 283–288 High Holborn
London WC1V 7HZ
www.kingfisherpub.com

This edition first published by
Kingfisher Publications Plc 2006
2 4 6 8 10 9 7 5 3 1

1TR/0706/TWP/UNV(PICA)/150ENSOMA/F

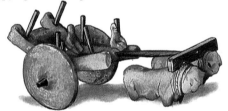

A CIP catalogue record for this book is
available from the British Library

ISBN-10: 0 7534 1401 5
ISBN-13: 978 0 7534 1401 9

Author: Hazel Mary Martell
Consultant: Dr Paul Bahn
Editors: Cynthia O'Neill, Ruth Nason, Catherine Headlam
Designers: Shaun Barlow, Ch'en Ling, Terry Woodley,
Karin Ambrose, John Jamieson
Art editor: Val Wright
Picture research: Su Alexander, Elaine Willis
Typesetters: Tracey McNerney, SPAN of Lingfield, Surrey
Printed in Singapore

THE
ANCIENT
WORLD

FROM T... ...ROME

❖ CONTENTS ❖

INTRODUCTION

From the time of the first people to the end of the 6th century AD, many cultures developed in different parts of the world. Some were short-lived. Others lasted almost unchanged for centuries. They left various kinds of evidence of their existence, which archaeologists examine and explain, to give us a picture of everyday life far back in ancient times.

Archaeologists dig up ancient sites and make a scientific study of what they find. This includes artefacts, such as tools, weapons, vehicles, clothing and jewellery, and features, such as the remains of buildings, streets and earthworks. Equally important are the ecofacts found at all sites.

◆ *A Danish woman fully preserved in a peat bog around AD 95 provides good information.*

◆ *Archaeologists digging up, or excavating, a site. Each layer of soil is carefully searched for remains from the past.*

Ecofacts are the remains of plants and animals. They give clues to what the environment was like at a particular time, and also to diet, cooking methods and even occupations.

Archaeologists sometimes also find the remains of human bodies and, by studying the bones and teeth, can estimate a person's gender and the age at which he or she died. The bones also contain clues to some diseases, such as arthritis, from which the person might have suffered. Some bones show evidence of breaks and other injuries which in turn reveal how people lived and died and how they were looked after if they were hurt.

♦ *These sea monsters are petroglyphs, which is the archaeologists' word for rock carvings. They were done by the prehistoric Nootka Indians and are found near Sproat Lake in British Columbia, Canada.*

Many of the objects excavated are things that people threw away or lost. In some cases, though, objects were deliberately buried with the dead to help them in the next life. As these grave goods often included valuable gold or silver items, many graves were robbed soon after the burial and it is unusual to find this kind of evidence.

Rock paintings and carvings are other evidence of life in the ancient world. Portraits and statues give clues about appearance and dress. Some cultures made clay models to bury with the dead, showing people at work, houses, boats and even pigsties.

Coins discovered at a site, showing the head and name of a known ruler, can help archaeologists to date their finds. They also look for changes in styles of some artefacts to identify a date. This method is known as typology. Wooden objects up to 8,000 years old can be dated by dendrochronology, or tree ring dating. Radiocarbon dating is used for even older wood and other once living material, including bones. Pottery can be dated using thermoluminescence. Dendrochronology, radiocarbon dating and thermoluminescence are all included in the glossary of terms on pages 145–147.

There are difficulties with written evidence of the ancient world. Some is in languages which no one today can decipher. Myths, legends and history become mixed and so no one can be sure that everything written is exactly true. Nonetheless, written evidence can add to our understanding of ancient civilizations. Sometimes we even find personal details, as in the letter from a Roman mother to her soldier son at Hadrian's Wall, telling him she was sending him underwear and socks.

♦ *These letters are from the Vindolanda fort, just south of Hadrian's Wall in Britain. They are inviting people to a birthday party, and were written around the beginning of the 2nd century AD.*

PIECING HISTORY TOGETHER

The artefacts and features that archaeologists discover at an ancient site represent only a small part of what was originally there. Items made from wood, cloth and leather have often rotted away. Stone buildings have been pulled down by later generations who wanted the stone for their own purposes. Some sites have been built over many times since they were first occupied and some of their secrets are only revealed by rescue archaeology when present-day buildings are demolished and new foundations are dug.

◆ *A Persian artefact dating from the 5th century BC. It is a gold drinking cup probably used by a Persian king.*

Peoples such as the Australian Aborigines and the Native Americans, who lived in harmony with their environment and passed their knowledge on by word of mouth, left little archaeological and no written evidence. Because of this, historians in the 19th and early 20th centuries often described them as uncivilized, even though their way of life had lasted much longer than that of the Greeks or Romans.

Dating events in ancient times is difficult and not all dates given are precise. When dates are approximate, this is shown by the letter *c.*, short for *circa* (meaning 'around'). Other letters you see with dates in this book are BC (before Christ) and AD (*anno Domini*, meaning 'in the year of the Lord'). This system ties in with the calendar of the Christian religion, with year 1 being the year Jesus Christ was said to be born. (Historians now think he was born five years earlier, *c.* 5 BC.) Other religions have their own calendars and number their years differently.

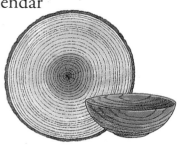

◆ *Tree rings can be used to help date wooden objects. This system of dating is called dendrochronology.*

◆ *A paleontologist (dinosaur expert) carefully dusts the earth from a dinosaur skeleton.*

In the 19th century archaeologists in Europe divided the past according to what people used to make tools and weapons. This gave the Stone Age, Bronze Age and Iron Age. The labels worked well in Europe, where people progressed from stone to bronze to iron at roughly the same times, but were inappropriate in other parts of the world. For example, the Ancient

Chinese used bronze long before the Europeans. Many Africans went straight from stone tools to iron ones, and the Americans used metals only for ornaments, and made everything else from stone.

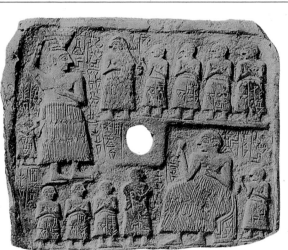

◆ *A stone relief found in Mesopotamia shows scribes being taught their craft.*

Apart from the next chapter, which looks at events worldwide, this book is arranged geographically. Each chapter tells the story of a different region, such as Ancient Egypt or the Indus Valley. Remember that the cultures in several of these regions were in existence at the same time. For example, while the Egyptians were building their pyramids, people in Britain were building Stonehenge and people in Peru were farming on terraces and growing cotton and potatoes. People from different cultures met through trade and, more often, through war and conflict. Floods, droughts and increases in population caused some people to migrate and their way of life adapted to their new surroundings.

In the chronology on pages 148–151, you will find a quick guide to what was happening at any one time throughout the ancient world.

◆ *Taking photographs from above the ground can reveal evidence that would have been difficult to identify on the ground. This is the remains of a Celtic hill fort in Ireland.*

◆ *Archaeological finds can capture the public interest. This Italian newspaper shows the excitement people felt when Howard Carter unearthed the pharaoh Tutankhamun's tomb.*

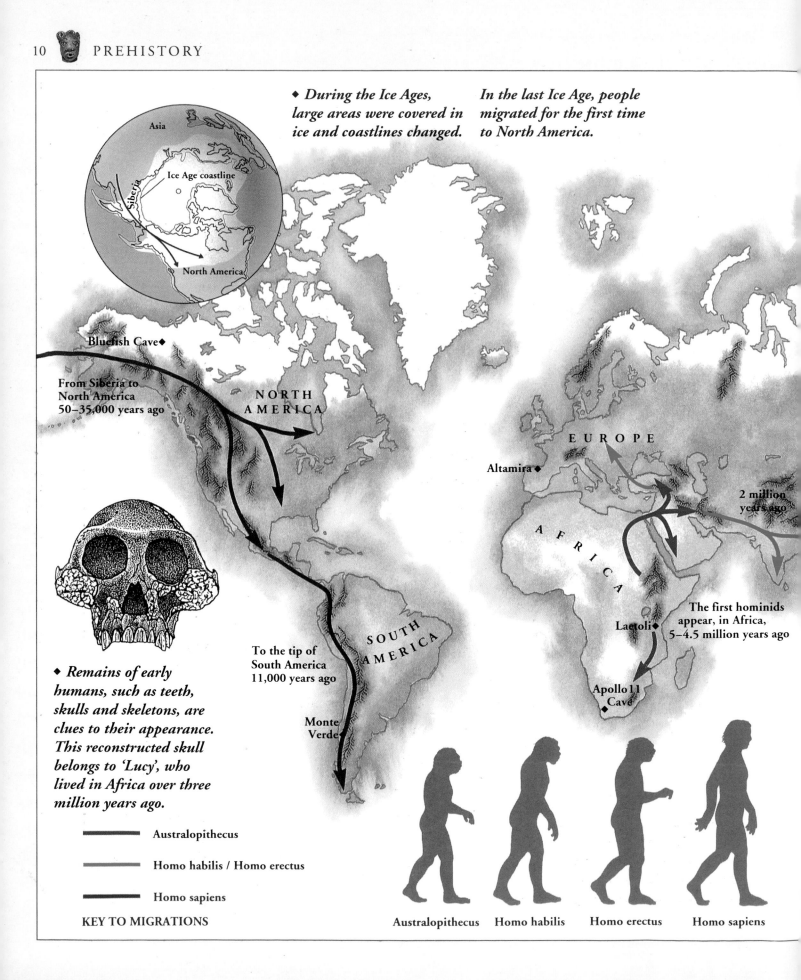

During the Ice Ages, large areas were covered in ice and coastlines changed.

In the last Ice Age, people migrated for the first time to North America.

Asia

Siberia

Ice Age coastline

North America

Bluefish Cave◆

From Siberia to North America 50–35,000 years ago

NORTH AMERICA

◆ Remains of early humans, such as teeth, skulls and skeletons, are clues to their appearance. This reconstructed skull belongs to 'Lucy', who lived in Africa over three million years ago.

To the tip of South America 11,000 years ago

SOUTH AMERICA

Monte Verde

EUROPE

Altamira ◆

2 million years ago

AFRICA

The first hominids appear, in Africa, 5–4.5 million years ago

Laetoli ◆

Apollo 11 Cave
◆

——— Australopithecus

——— Homo habilis / Homo erectus

——— Homo sapiens

KEY TO MIGRATIONS

Australopithecus   Homo habilis   Homo erectus   Homo sapiens

◆ *A hollow bone pierced with holes is one of the earliest known musical instruments. Teeth and tiny bones formed a necklace. These were both made by* Homo sapiens.

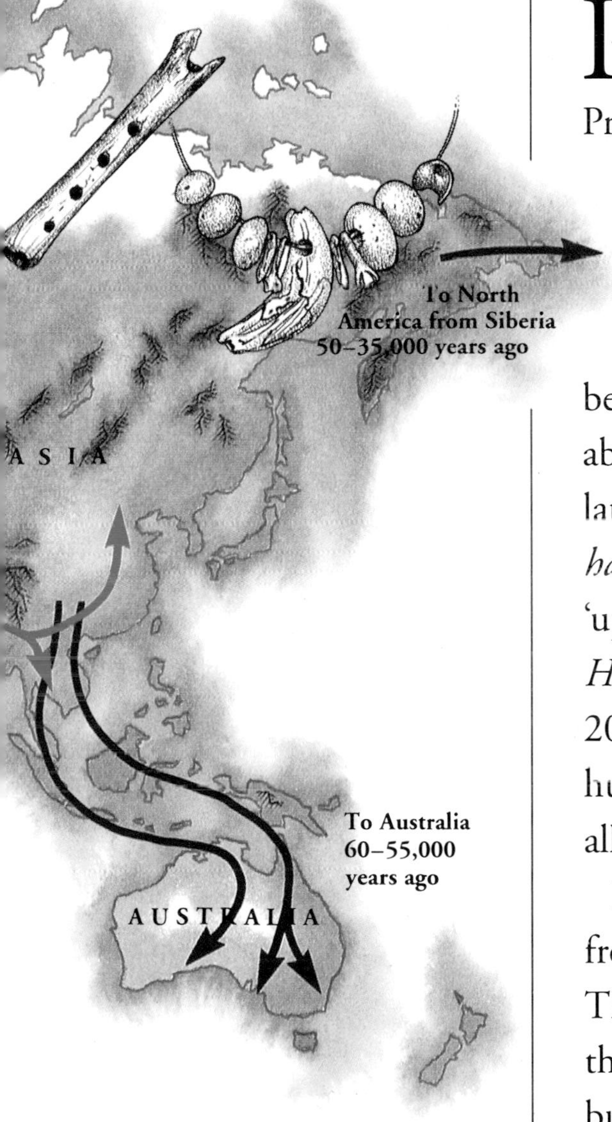

To North
America from Siberia
50–35,000 years ago

ASIA

To Australia
60–55,000
years ago

AUSTRALIA

◆ *Prehistoric humans evolved over millions of years, gradually spreading across the world. The four main groups are shown to the left.*

PREHISTORY

Prehistory is often defined as the time before there were written records. This chapter on Prehistory, however, concentrates on the story of humans from the time of the first hominids to the end of the last Ice Age.

Australopithecines are the earliest known hominids. Their fossilized remains have been found in Tanzania, Africa, the oldest being about four million years old. Two million years later, the first true humans appeared, *Homo habilis*, or 'handy human'. *Homo erectus*, or 'upright human', appeared 300,000 years later. *Homo sapiens*, or 'wise human', started to flourish 200,000 years ago and were much more like the humans of today, *Homo sapiens sapiens*. Their skills allowed them to spread throughout the world.

Many of the earliest remains from this period are fossils. Through careful study of them, researchers have built up a picture of human evolution.

THE PEOPLE OF THE ICE AGE

UP TO 8000 BC

Homo sapiens gathered nuts and berries and hunted animals for food. They killed smaller animals with spears, and trapped large ones in holes covered with brushwood. In warm places such as Africa these people did not need clothes, but once they moved to cooler areas they made garments for themselves.

One group known as the Neanderthals, after the valley in Germany where many of their remains have been found, was particularly successful at living in cool climates. By 70,000 BC they were living throughout Europe and in parts of Asia. They used stone knives to remove an animal's skin, scrape the flesh off it, and then cut it into shapes. With a stone point they punched holes along the edges of the pieces, and joined them together with thread made from sinew, pulling it through with a bone needle.

For shelter, *Homo sapiens* first used caves and overhanging rocks. Later, with improved tools, they cut down tree branches to make frames for skin tents. Many of them lived a nomadic life, following herds of animals all year round. *Homo sapiens*, however, probably spent most of their time in one small area.

All *Homo sapiens* knew how to make fire, either by rotating one piece of wood against another or by chipping two hard stones together to make sparks. They caught the sparks on a handful of dried grass to make a flame.

These were the first humans to bury their dead with grave goods, including meat and tools. This suggests that they believed in another life after death.

By about 35,000 BC, the Neanderthals had started to be replaced by the Cro-Magnons, named after a site in France where their remains have been found. They probably came to Europe from the Near East and, from about 27,000 BC, they painted pictures of animals deep inside some

◆ *These footprints were found in Laetoli, Tanzania. They were made in volcanic ash which later hardened after a shower of rain. They are nearly four million years old.*

◆ Homo sapiens *made tools by chipping off pieces from one stone with another. Tools included axes, knives, scrapers, borers and spearheads.*

caves, evidence perhaps of a belief in magic or nature gods.

Life changed dramatically during the most recent Ice Age, which began about 100,000 years ago and reached its coldest period between 23,000 BC and 14,000 BC. The polar icecaps expanded, covering large areas of Europe, Asia and North America in thick ice. Vast amounts of water which would usually have flowed into rivers and seas were frozen up in the ice and so sea levels fell worldwide. Coastlines changed, and some places which had been separated by water became joined by land.

Many plants and animals could not survive where they were and either died out or migrated. Reindeer moved as far south as northern Spain, while woolly mammoths and woolly rhinoceroses became common in northern areas where forests had been replaced by the cold, open steppe. People, too, migrated.

♦ Homo sapiens *used fire to keep warm, frighten away predators and cook food. They sewed skins together using needles made from bone.*

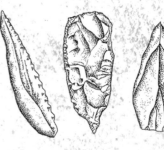

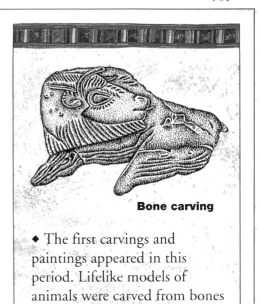

Bone carving

♦ The first carvings and paintings appeared in this period. Lifelike models of animals were carved from bones and antlers.

Mammoth bone shelter

♦ There were few trees on the steppes of northern Europe, and so mammoth bones were sometimes used instead of branches for the framework of shelters.

Stone tools

♦ Sharp tools such as knives or scrapers were made from stone and flint.

MIGRATING AND SETTLING DOWN

UP TO 8000 BC

Both *Homo erectus* and *Homo sapiens* were on the move long before the last Ice Age started. Many different reasons led them to migrate. Sometimes the population of an area increased to such a point that there was not enough food for everybody. In other cases, a natural disaster, such as a flood or a drought, made it impossible for people to continue living in an area. Some people might have moved simply out of a sense of adventure.

The approach of the Ice Age forced populations in the coldest regions to move to areas where they would have a better chance of survival. Another effect

of the expanding ice was to make possible some of the longest of the early migrations.

For example, as more and more water became trapped in the ice, the sea between southeast Asia and Australia became small and shallow enough for people to sail across it. By about 53,000 BC, therefore, people arrived in and started to inhabit Australia.

As the sea level dropped still

farther, land appeared between Asia and North America. This made it possible for people from Asia to walk across and start to inhabit land where humans had never lived before.

RETURN OF THE SEAS
Once the temperatures started to rise again, the ice melted and the seas returned. The Americas were once more cut off by water. In Europe, Britain became an island as the land bridge which had joined it to the mainland disappeared under the Straits of Dover.

When the Ice Age ended, many of the plants and animals which had flourished in the cold became extinct. People who had relied on them for food now had to change their way of life.

◆ *People who crossed from Asia to America at the height of the Ice Age had to wait until the ice started to melt before they could move farther south. Even then the journey must have been perilous, as it was still very cold and there was always the threat of attack by wild animals.*

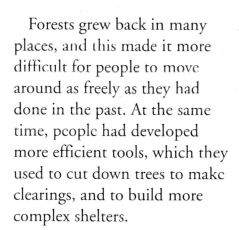

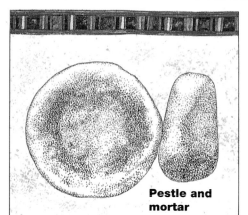

Pestle and mortar

◆ People had started to settle in the village of Monte Verde, in southern Chile, by 11,000 BC. They made their houses of timber frames covered with the hides of mastodons, a kind of elephant, and lived by hunting and gathering.

◆ In some places grain crops such as wheat and barley grew in the wild. People gathered them when they were ripe, took the grains and ground them into flour using a pestle and mortar.

Forests grew back in many places, and this made it more difficult for people to move around as freely as they had done in the past. At the same time, people had developed more efficient tools, which they used to cut down trees to make clearings, and to build more complex shelters.

Once this happened, people began to lead more settled lives. They still hunted animals and gathered fruits and berries, but perhaps they now moved only between two settlements, depending on the season of the year. The settlements were more permanent and, in some parts of the world, the condition of the land and the weather was right for people to start farming.

Slotted fish spear

◆ Early people developed more efficient weapons to help them hunt for food. The fish spear was grooved with barbs made of flint, making it hard to dislodge. The arrowhead was held in place with sinew.

◆ During this period the first recognizable statues of people appeared. They are mostly of women and may represent some sort of fertility goddess.

Ivory carving of a head made over 24,000 years ago

◆ More than 200 decorated caves have been found in Europe. The paintings date from 30-10,000 years ago. This bison is on the ceiling of a cave in Altamira, Spain. Art from the same period exists on every other continent.

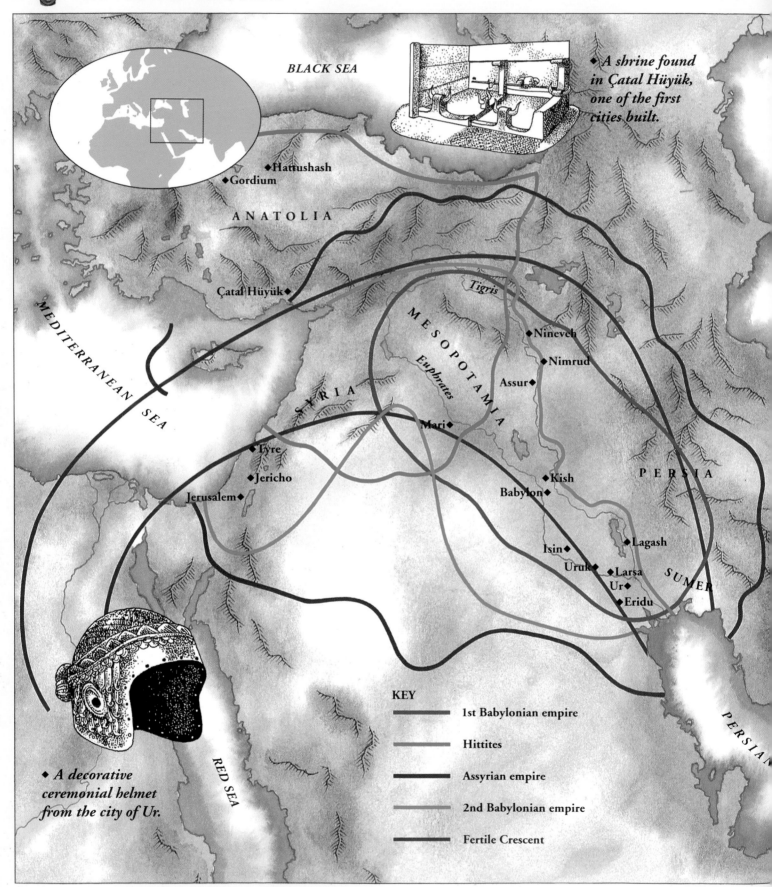

BLACK SEA

◆ *A shrine found in Çatal Hüyük, one of the first cities built.*

◆Hattushash
◆Gordium

A N A T O L I A

Çatal Hüyük◆

MEDITERRANEAN SEA

Tigris

M E S O P O T A M I A

Euphrates

◆Nineveh
◆Nimrud
Assur◆

S Y R I A

Mari◆

◆Tyre
◆Jericho
Jerusalem◆

◆Kish
Babylon◆

P E R S I A

Isin◆
Uruk◆
◆Lagash
◆Larsa
Ur◆
◆Eridu

S U M E R

RED SEA

◆ *A decorative ceremonial helmet from the city of Ur.*

PERSIAN

KEY

——— 1st Babylonian empire

——— Hittites

——— Assyrian empire

——— 2nd Babylonian empire

——— Fertile Crescent

THE FERTILE CRESCENT

Some of the earliest known civilizations developed in an area known as the Fertile Crescent. This stretched in an arc shape, from the northern end of the Persian Gulf to the valley of the Nile River in Egypt.

The Fertile Crescent was an ideal place for people to settle and start farming, because wheat and barley, sheep and goats were all found there in the wild. Once groups of people began to settle, they could grow more crops than they needed. So while some people farmed, others developed crafts and trade. They also devised systems of writing.

Villages, towns and cities sprang up as the population grew. In some places, ancient towns appear as large mounds, or tells, where new buildings were constructed on the ruins of earlier ones. Excavating from the top downwards, archaeologists have built up pictures of life in the Fertile Crescent over many centuries.

♦ The walls of the city Hattushash, which was the Hittite capital from about 1650 BC.

FIRST FARMERS AND FIRST CITIES

c. 10,000–5000 BC

The first people in the Fertile Crescent hunted wild animals for meat and gathered nuts, seeds, fruit and grain to complete their diet. In time, farming developed from this way of life.

KEEPING ANIMALS

Dogs were tamed from wolves and used in hunting and herding wild animals. Gradually, goats, sheep and pigs were also domesticated, as were wild cattle. These were probably from a breed called aurochs, fierce and dangerous and much bigger than cattle today. They were probably kept for meat rather than milk.

The soil in the Fertile Crescent was light and easy to dig with simple tools, and there was enough sunshine and rainfall for crops to grow and ripen each year. The first farmers gathered wild wheat and barley seeds and planted them in soil which they had dug over with digging sticks and hoes. They harvested the grain with wooden sickles, which had a cutting edge made from flint or obsidian.

Because people were now leading settled lives, they could harvest all the grain they had grown and store it. They could also try to develop better crops and better animals, by breeding from the best.

CITIES

Some farming settlements eventually grew into the first cities. The oldest excavated so far is ancient Jericho, by the Jordan River. The permanent water supply and warm climate made it possible to grow enough food to support a large population. People first settled there from around 9000 BC, and by 8000 BC the community was organized enough to build a stone wall to defend the city. Houses were built of mud bricks, with flat timber roofs.

Another ancient city is Çatal Hüyük, at the northern end of the Fertile Crescent in what is now Turkey. The site dates from around 7000 BC. By 6250 BC, about 6,000 people lived there.

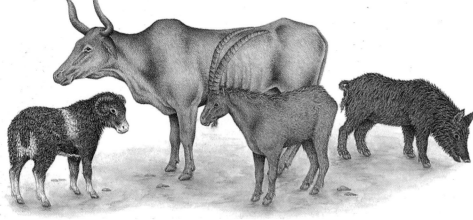

◆ *The cattle, sheep, goats and pigs bred by the early farmers were usually smaller and skinnier than those of today. They were also hairier and had bigger horns.*

◆ *The walls at Çatal Hüyük were smoothly plastered, and some were painted with leopards, bulls and people. They may have been shrines to various gods. One painting shows birds attacking a headless body. It probably represents the local custom of exposing dead bodies to the elements, before burying them under platforms in the houses.*

The houses were made from mud bricks. No streets separated the houses. People walked along the rooftops and down a ladder through a hole in the roof to enter their home.

Here people ate apples, almonds and pistachio nuts, as well as wheat, peas and beef. They used obsidian for mirrors, tools and weapons, and shells from the Mediterranean, which they used to make jewellery.

◆ *Date palms were very useful to the early farmers. As well as eating the fruit, they could roof their houses with the leaves, and plait or weave them to make ropes, mats and sandals. The tree trunks provided timber.*

◆ Early farmers grew wild wheat and barley. At some time, wild wheat crossed naturally with a kind of grass. The new wheat had plump seeds. People discovered that grinding the seeds between two stones, called querns, produced flour to make a new kind of food: bread.

Wheat **Barley**

◆ The bricks for the early houses were made from mud or clay. They were shaped by hand and left to bake in the sun until they were hard enough to use for building.

Sun-baked mud brick

◆ A figure found in one of the shrines at Çatal Hüyük may have been a mother goddess. But very little is known about the religion of this time.

Clay figurine of a woman

MESOPOTAMIA AND SUMER

5000–2000 BC

Mesopotamia means 'between two rivers', referring to the fertile plain between the Tigris and Euphrates Rivers, in what is now Iraq. From about 5500 BC the region was settled by a people we call the Sumerians.

Although the climate was dry and rainfall unreliable, the rivers allowed early farmers to set up irrigation systems to water the crops of barley, wheat, sesame and onions. Ditches were dug to carry water from the rivers to the fields of growing crops.

Farming villages grew up and the population expanded. By about 3500 BC, some villages had developed into cities, such as Ur, Eridu, Lagash, Kish and Babylon. Each was a home for thousands of people.

These cities were in the southern part of Mesopotamia, an area which is sometimes called Sumer. Each city had its own ruler and this ruler had control over the land around the city. Because of this expanded area, each city was known as a city-state.

Rivalry often sprang up between the cities. In 2360 BC Sargon, the king of Kish, united the cities of Akkad, a region north of Sumer. He then conquered the Sumerian city-states and and went on to control, briefly, the first Mesopotamian empire.

By 2100 BC, however, Ur had taken over as the most important city in Mesopotamia.

◆ *The Sumerians invented the wheel, but probably first used it for making pottery. We know that they had carts with solid wooden wheels by about 3000 BC.*

◆ *The ziggurat at Ur was completed in about 2100 BC. It was built of sun-baked clay bricks. Religious ceremonies and sacrifices took place in the temple at the top.*

◆ *Sumerian princesses dressed in colourful clothes and headdresses. Their jewellery was made from gold, silver and coloured stones such as lapis lazuli and cornelians.*

PALACES AND ZIGGURATS

Each city had a royal palace for its ruler and fine public buildings. In the centre was a mound, or ziggurat, on top of which stood a temple for the god who protected the city. Around the ziggurat, houses were closely packed together along narrow, winding streets.

Priests and priestesses served in the temple, and officials kept records of its property. The temple owned most of the land and livestock in the city.

The need to keep records led to the development of writing on clay tablets by 3100 BC, and thousands of these still exist today. They record details of many areas of Sumerian life, from medical instructions to military victories.

The clay tablets also include a poem called *The Epic of Gilgamesh* which tells a story of a flood, similar to the story of Noah's Ark found in the Bible. The hero, Gilgamesh, was a Sumerian king who lived around 2600 BC.

CRAFTS AND TRADE

Many craftworkers lived in the cities. They were highly skilled in metal- and stonework. Examples of their art, including musical instruments, jewellery, vases and carvings, have been excavated from the royal tombs at Ur.

Trade also flourished. The main export was finely woven woollen cloth. Sumerian ships sailed to lands around the Persian Gulf to buy ivory. Merchants and traders came to the region to sell goods from as far away as the Indus Valley, Afghanistan and Persia.

Cuneiform tablet

◆ *Sumerian writing consisted of triangular marks, which were made by pressing a wedge-shaped tip into wet clay. This is known as cuneiform writing, from the Latin word* cuneus *which means 'wedge'.*

◆ Reeds were so plentiful on the riverbanks in Mesopotamia that the Sumerians were able to use them to build their houses. The Marsh Arabs who live on the banks of the Tigris River still build their houses this way.

Reed house

Decorated lyre, Ur

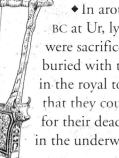

◆ In around 2500 BC at Ur, lyre players were sacrificed and buried with their lyres in the royal tombs, so that they could play for their dead masters in the underworld.

◆ Among the treasures excavated from the temple at Uruk was a vase, showing fruits of the harvest being given to a female figure: either a priestess, or Inanna, the goddess of fertility.

Carved scenes from an alabaster vase, Uruk

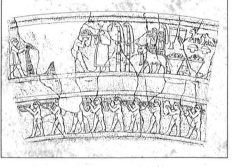

MESOPOTAMIA AND BABYLON

2000–1155 BC

Ur reached the height of its importance in about 2000 BC, when it was the richest, most powerful city in Mesopotamia. Around 20,000 people are thought to have lived there, under the rule of King Ur-Nammu. His strong army and efficient civil service helped him run his empire from Uruk as well as Ur. Babylon, the city-state 300 kilometres northwest of Ur, was part of this empire.

Babylon's rise to power began during the 19th century BC. At this time, Ur's wealth and importance were declining, partly because of the disappearance of the Indus Valley civilization with which Ur had traded. King Sumuabum (who ruled 1894–1881 BC) declared Babylon's independence from Ur and set up a dynasty which lasted almost 300 years.

The sixth ruler, Hammurabi the Great, came to power in 1792 BC. He was an efficient leader, with strong, well-disciplined armies. Under him Babylon expanded its territory by conquering all of Sumer and

Hammurabi

Hammurabi had his code of laws carved on to a stone stela. The carving at the top shows him standing with the Sun god Shamash, who is holding a ring and a staff.

◆ *Wealthy Babylonians lived in flat-roofed houses, with balconies and an open courtyard. Servants cleaned and cooked for them: recipes from the time mention 20 different cheeses and 100 varieties of soup.*

Akkad, including the city-states of Isin, Elam and Larsa, as well as the kingdom of Mari on the Euphrates River.

In spite of his wars of conquest, Hammurabi brought prosperity and peace to the Babylonians. Increased trade with Persia brought more wealth. The power of the priests declined. Unlike previous rulers, Hammurabi did not think of himself as a god. Instead, he called himself 'the favourite of the gods'.

Hammurabi set out a new code of laws for his people to follow. There were 282 laws in all. They were often harsh, but they did recognize the fact that a person might kill or injure someone accidentally, as well as on purpose. The laws also gave some status to women and protected their property rights.

Hammurabi died in 1750 BC. Weak kings followed, and Babylon finally collapsed in 1595 BC, when it was raided by Mursilis, the Hittite king. After this, a people called the Kassites ruled the city-state, until about 1155 BC.

◆ *The Babylonians had time to play games, including this one with a marked board, dice and counters. Unfortunately, no rules survive, so we do not know how it was played.*

◆ Hammurabi's laws were made to protect the weak. They covered all aspects of daily life, such as rates of pay for hiring transport and rules for trading. They also set out penalties for wrongdoers. A man who broke another's leg would have his own leg broken as punishment. Kidnappers, burglars, bandits and witches were put to death.

Hammurabi

◆ Land was owned by kings, temples and individuals. It could also be rented, sold or given away. Royal grants of land were recorded on boundary stones, together with carvings of local gods and inscribed prayers asking them to protect the land.

Boundary stone, Babylon

◆ Babylonian mathematicians devised a counting system based on the number 60. We still use it today when measuring time in seconds and minutes. The system was useful to traders and astronomers, because 60 can be divided quite easily.

THE HITTITES AND THE ASSYRIANS

2000–609 BC

◆ *The warlike Hittites were well known for their skilled use of the chariot in battle.*

The Hittites appeared in Anatolia from the northeast, at the start of the second millennium BC. By 1750 BC, they controlled the main cities in the area. They were made up of several tribes, speaking as many as six languages. The most important was probably Neshite, because this was used to record their history on clay tablets.

The Hittite capital was formed at Hattushash in Anatolia in the 17th century BC. The Hittites later conquered Babylon, Mesopotamia and northern Syria. They were at their peak from about 1400 BC, and unsuccessfully tried to conquer Egypt in the 13th century BC. The Hittite empire suddenly collapsed about 1200 BC and was overwhelmed by migrants from Thrace in southern Europe who established their own kingdom.

THE ASSYRIANS

The Assyrians were an Aramaic-speaking people, who eventually came to dominate northern Mesopotamia. They had settled in the valley of the Tigris River by 2000 BC, and built a capital at Assur. The city became part of the Mesopotamian empire in 1800 BC, but soon regained its independence.

◆ *The magnificent royal palace at Nimrud showed foreign visitors the might of the Assyrian empire under the king, Assurnasirpal II, in the 9th century BC.*

◆ *The Assyrians were skilled at siege warfare. To attack city walls, they used battering rams and scaling ladders.*

Assyrian stone carving

◆ Most Assyrian stone carvings are of the rulers and their conquests, but some show scenes of everyday life, such as preparing and cooking food.

◆ Both the Hittites and the Assyrians kept slaves. Some were probably people they had captured in battle, but Assyrian men also sold their wives and children into slavery, in order to pay off their debts.

◆ The Hittites had many gods. They also believed that their kings represented the gods on Earth, and became gods themselves when they died.

Gold figure of a Hittite king, from about 1400 BC

By the 14th century BC, the Assyrian territory had grown to include the area around Nineveh, a large city on the banks of the Tigris. This expansion continued under King Adadnirari I, who ruled from 1298 BC. He and the kings who succeeded him were dictators and their conquered subjects often rebelled against them as the empire grew.

From around 1100 BC, other Aramaic peoples took control of Assyria. They were beaten back a hundred years later by Assurdan II, who continued to expand the Assyrian empire. By 650 BC it stretched from Syria to the Persian Gulf and included Babylon and most of Egypt. Assurbanipal was the last great king. He was a sponsor of the arts and built up a vast library at his palace in Nineveh. After his death, the empire began to collapse and by 609 BC, it had ended.

THE CHALDEANS AND BABYLON

626–539 BC

The Chaldeans were a tribe of people who migrated into Assyria and Babylonia from around 1100 BC. They were attracted by the rich and fertile land and at first settled around Ur. From there many of them moved to Babylon. A hundred years later, when Assurdan II re-established the Assyrian empire, the Chaldeans in Babylon were important enough to be made kings of Babylon, under Assyrian overlords. Babylon's power then started to grow again, so that in 626 BC King Nabopolassar declared Babylonia independent of the Assyrians.

A new Babylonian empire was established under King Nebuchadnezzar II (605-562 BC). He was a warlike king whose reign was marked by military campaigns, including one against Egypt.

Syria, Phoenicia, Judah, and also Assyria which was conquered with the help of the Medes, became part of Nebuchadnezzar's empire. Revolts against him were put down ruthlessly, as when he besieged the Phoenician port of Tyre for 13 years. He also captured Jerusalem where he destroyed much of the city

◆ Babylon must have been an impressive sight for people approaching from the north. Having passed through the Ishtar Gate, which was flanked by two fortresses, they would have been greeted by a view of the famous Hanging Gardens.

◆ *The Ishtar Gate is the only well-preserved surviving monument from Babylon. It was decorated with glazed bricks, showing dragons which represented the chief god Marduk and bulls which symbolized the storm god Adad.*

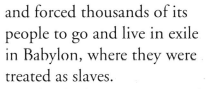

and forced thousands of its people to go and live in exile in Babylon, where they were treated as slaves.

Nebuchadnezzar improved cities in his empire, making Babylon especially more beautiful and more secure. He had built a palace for himself, a temple to the god Marduk and a huge new city wall. Its main gate was named after the goddess Ishtar. He also created the Hanging Gardens, which were acclaimed as one of the seven wonders of the ancient world.

The Greek writer Herodotus said that

◆ *The Assyrians had thought of Ishtar as the goddess of war, but to the Babylonians she was a mother goddess who helped to protect the city.*

the city of Babylon was built in a square which measured 22 kilometres on each side. It was divided by the Euphrates River which flowed between two walls of brick. Where the ends of streets met these walls, there were large bronze gates to give people access to the river. Merchants and traders could sail their ships from the Persian Gulf, up the Euphrates and right into the city.

Nebuchadnezzar was succeeded in 562 BC by his son, Awil-Marduk, who was assassinated three years later. After three more years and two more kings, Babylonian power collapsed completely. A Syrian prince, Nabu-Na'id, seized power until 539 BC, when Babylon was invaded by the Persians and Babylonia became part of the Persian empire.

◆ Nebuchadnezzar built the Hanging Gardens for his wife Amytis because she missed the hills of her own country, Persia. Plants and trees from Persia were planted and slaves carried up water for them from the Euphrates.

Nebuchadnezzar

◆ Nebuchadnezzar was anxious to keep alive the links with the first Babylonian empire. He encouraged everybody to worship Marduk and always used the old Sumerian script for writing.

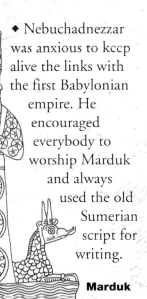

Marduk

◆ To try to ensure fair trade, Babylon had a system of weights. This one below is in the shape of a duck.

Babylonian weight

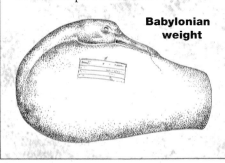

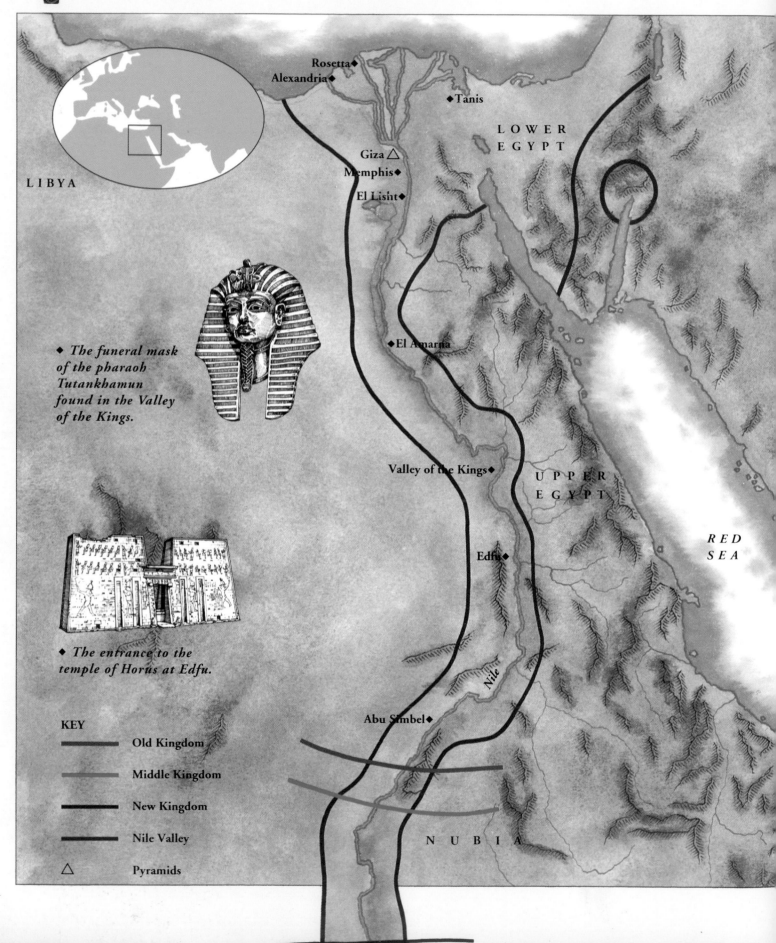

LIBYA

Rosetta◆

Alexandria◆

◆ Tanis

LOWER
EGYPT

Giza △

Memphis◆

El Lisht◆

◆ *The funeral mask
of the pharaoh
Tutankhamun
found in the Valley
of the Kings.*

◆ El Amarna

Valley of the Kings◆

UPPER
EGYPT

RED
SEA

Edfu◆

Nile

◆ *The entrance to the
temple of Horus at Edfu.*

Abu Simbel◆

KEY

———— Old Kingdom

———— Middle Kingdom

———— New Kingdom

———— Nile Valley

△ Pyramids

NUBIA

◆ *The pyramids of Giza. The largest of these, the Great Pyramid, was built for Khufu and finished around 2528 BC.*

ANCIENT EGYPT

From mid-July to October each year, the Nile River flooded, leaving a layer of silt along the riverbanks and so turning desert into land where crops could grow. The floods made it possible for a civilization to grow up in ancient Egypt.

The communities along the Nile developed into two separate states by the fourth millennium BC, each ruled by a king. Lower Egypt occupied the Nile Delta, while Upper Egypt stretched south for about 800 kilometres. In about 3100 BC, King Menes of Upper Egypt conquered Lower Egypt and united the two.

Following this, the history of ancient Egypt is divided into three main periods: the Old Kingdom, the Middle Kingdom and the New Kingdom. In each period, the Egyptians were intensely concerned with death and the afterlife. The remains of their tombs, together with written records, have helped archaeologists build up a detailed picture of what Egyptian life was like.

ANCIENT EGYPT: THE OLD KINGDOM

3100–2040 BC

When King Menes united Upper and Lower Egypt in around 3100 BC, the new nation was already rich, thanks to the Nile River and the abundant sunshine. It was easy to grow crops in the fertile soil by the riverbank. People planted barley and wheat to make bread and beer, as well as flax, from which they made linen for clothes. They caught fish, hunted wildfowl on the marshes and picked wild fruits and vegetables.

Menes made his capital at Memphis in the former Lower Egypt, from where he ruled the whole country. He was helped by 42 nomarchs, each of whom governed a province of Egypt on his behalf. They made sure that his commands were obeyed.

The growth of cities and a centralized government encouraged the use of writing. For instance, government records were written on sheets of papyrus. The first known textbook on surgery was put together at this time. Further advances came when people studied the Nile and devised systems of irrigation to take advantage of its floods. With careful irrigation, they could grow two crops a year.

The dynasties, or ruling families, of Egypt are numbered from the time of King Menes. Ancient Egyptian history is divided into the Archaic period and the Old, Middle and New Kingdom periods, with Intermediary periods in between.

◆ *The ancient Egyptians kept cattle as working animals as well as for meat. The animals worked on the land, but were often taken to help on a building project while the fields were flooded.*

◆ *It took thousands of men many years to build a pyramid. Each stone had to be quarried, brought to the site and then pulled or pushed up a long ramp as the pyramid grew higher.*

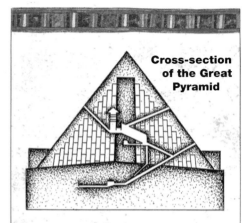

Cross-section of the Great Pyramid

PYRAMID BUILDERS

The Old Kingdom started with the 4th dynasty in 2575 BC. It was in this time that belief in the afterlife became an important part of Egyptian religion, although at first only the king was thought to have a real life after death. Mastabas (flat-topped tombs with sloping sides) were built for the bodies of dead pharaohs and important nobles. The mastabas were followed by step-sided pyramids and, later still, the true smooth-sided pyramids.

The Egyptians had many different gods, but the most important was the Sun god, Re, whose main temple was at Heliopolis. Re was the creator god.

The Old Kingdom lasted for over 400 years, until a series of low floods led to a drought, which, in turn, led to half a century of famine. At the same time, the nomarchs became more powerful and independent. In 2134 BC the Old Kingdom collapsed and Egypt split into separate provinces, each with its own ruler.

◆ *Egyptian scribes used a form of picture writing, with about 700 different hieroglyphs. There was also a shorthand version, which was used for writing documents.*

◆ The Great Pyramid at Giza was built with over two million blocks of stone, each weighing about two tonnes. It was finished in around 2528 BC for King Khufu. He was buried in a special chamber near the middle of the pyramid. The pyramids at Giza were one of the seven wonders of the ancient world.

◆ The crown of Upper Egypt was white and that of Lower Egypt was red. After Menes united the two states, the pharaohs wore a double crown.

◆ Grain was an important commodity in ancient Egypt. It could be traded for other goods, as well as used to pay taxes. An accurate balance for weighing it was therefore necessary.

Grain balance

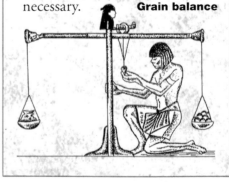

LIFE IN THE MIDDLE KINGDOM

2040–1550 BC

In 2040 BC the 11th dynasty king, Mentuhotep II, reunited Egypt. He ruled from Thebes, but his successors built a new royal capital at El Lisht. Helped by civil servants, pharaohs of the 11th and 12th dynasties took away control of Egypt from the nomarchs.

Trade continued along the Nile and trading contacts with the eastern Mediterranean and the Middle East were built up. To control this, the Egyptians conquered much of Nubia and built forts there for the armies occupying the new territory.

Increased trade and a time of peace brought wealth, and arts, crafts and literature flourished. People of the Old Kingdom had put great emphasis on respect for one's elders and for tradition. The people of the Middle Kingdom valued justice and fairness. Even so, the rule of the pharaohs was absolute.

♦ *Mummification involved drying out the body, rubbing it with cedar oil and stuffing it with linen and spices. It was then wrapped in linen bandages stiffened with resin. The coffin was painted with the dead person's portrait, so that its spirit would recognize it in the afterlife. Charms and amulets were often wrapped with the body to protect it from evil.*

Canopic jars

Embalmers removed the lungs, liver, stomach and intestines. They were dried out, put into containers called canopic jars, and placed in the tomb with the body.

♦ *The scene in an embalmer's workshop as a body is prepared for burial.*

TEMPLES AND GODS

Many new temples were built during the Middle Kingdom. Egyptians worshipped a number of different gods. Osiris, god of the Underworld, was most often worshipped. He was also the god of spring, who brought the seeds to life each year. People believed that, through him, they could share the afterlife. The bodies of all who could afford it were mummified on death.

INVASION

A series of weak rulers led to the collapse of the Middle Kingdom in 1640 BC. Lower Egypt was invaded by the Hyksos from Canaan. They introduced horse-drawn chariots, lutes and lyres, improved methods of spinning and weaving, and new weapons made from bronze, which were far more effective than the Egyptians' wooden weapons.

Civil servants visited each farm twice a year: once to estimate the crop and count the animals, and then to collect the tax, which was half of everything the farmer had produced.

According to mythology, Osiris and his wife Isis once ruled Egypt, but Osiris was killed by his jealous brother Seth, god of storms and violence, who wanted to rule Egypt himself. Seth scattered the pieces of Osiris's body throughout Egypt. Isis found the pieces and bandaged the body back together, making the first mummy.

◆ Wall paintings show us that Egyptians were fond of music, dancing and singing. Usually this was for entertainment, within the home or at a great feast.

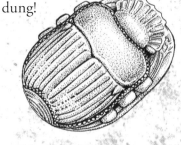

Little viol, with bow (Rebaba)

Oboe

Double clarinet

◆ Amulets, or protective charms, were important to the ancient Egyptians. The most popular were shaped like a beetle and represented the god Khepri, who was thought to push the Sun around in the same way that a beetle pushed a ball of dung!

Scarab beetle amulet

◆ In honour of the cat goddess Bastet, all cats in Egypt were thought sacred. Many were mummified when they died and some were then buried with their owners.

THE NEW KINGDOM: A GOLDEN AGE

1532–1070 BC

In 1532 BC the 18th dynasty pharaoh Ahmose defeated the Hyksos and reunited Egypt once more. This was the start of the New Kingdom, which is often looked on as the Golden Age of Egypt. As the country gained power, strong pharaohs were determined to create an empire. They led their armies to victory, conquering Palestine, Syria and all the lands west of the Euphrates River. As a result, rich gifts and tributes poured into Egypt, adding to the country's prosperity.

Many new temples were built at this time. Also, as the practice of burying pharaohs in pyramids had been abandoned, tombs were now cut for them in the cliffs of the Valley of the Kings.

POWER OF THE PHARAOHS

The pharaoh had total control of the country. Everybody and everything were thought to belong to him, and he could do whatever he wanted. One pharaoh who took advantage of this was Amenhotep IV. He introduced the worship of Aten,

◆ *Rameses II had two temples carved out of the cliffs at Abu Simbel. Both are watched over by carved figures of the pharaoh and his family. This temple is the smaller of the two.*

the Sun in the sky, and changed his own name to Akhenaten. Then he went so far as to change the religion of the country, saying that Aten was the only god and forcing people to abandon all others. He closed all the temples and used their wealth to create a new capital city for himself at Akhetaten, now El Amarna.

Akhenaten's beliefs were unpopular with ordinary people, and after his death his successor, Tutankhamun, brought back the old gods and made Thebes the capital once more.

Tutankhamun's Tomb

All pharaohs were buried with precious items, most of which were stolen later by grave robbers. Tutankhamun's tomb, however, survived almost intact until 1922, when archaeologists found it full of treasure, chariots, fine robes, musical instruments and furniture. This gold mask covered the face of the mummified 'boy king'. He was only 18 when he died.

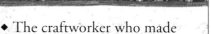

EVERYDAY LIFE

In spite of Egypt's wealth, most of the people were farmers and workers who still lived simple lives. The rich and the nobility, however, lived in luxury. They enjoyed a varied diet with plenty of meat, fruit and wine, instead of the bread and beer on which everyone else had to live. Their houses had little furniture, and were cool and airy. They often had bathrooms and shaded courtyards, containing shallow pools filled with fish.

The sons of noble families received an education in writing and arithmetic. In poor families children did not go to school, but went to work with their parents or helped out at home. Girls married at about twelve years of age and boys at 14.

Of 270 pharaohs, all but three or four were men. One of the exceptions was Queen Hatshepsut, who usurped the throne and ruled for 20 years. Women worked as priestesses, midwives, dancers, musicians and mourners. Some had market stalls and many helped their husbands on the farm.

◆ *The Egyptians developed a full-time army during the New Kingdom. Their swift war-chariots were pulled by two horses. Each chariot had a driver and a spearman or archer. Foot soldiers fought with swords, spears or bows and arrows.*

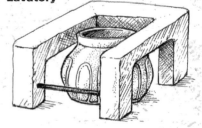

◆ The craftworker who made this fish-shaped bottle wrapped strips of coloured glass around the body and drew a point across them before the glass hardened, to make the ripples.

Fish-shaped scent bottle

◆ Cleanliness was important to the Egyptians. Many houses had a portable lavatory, consisting of a seat placed over a large jar filled with sand.

Lavatory

◆ The water clock was a jar marked with circles, equally far apart, which showed the passage of time. Water dripped through a hole in the bottom. Because the water came out faster when the jar was full, it had to be wider at the top than at the bottom.

Pottery water clock

THE END OF THE EGYPTIAN EMPIRE

1070–30 BC

Since the middle of the 12th century BC, the New Kingdom had been in decline. A scarcity of grain led to unrest in the country, which was also under threat of invasion by the Sea People. They were defeated by Rameses III (1194–1163 BC), but the pharaohs who followed him were less powerful.

By 1100 BC there was civil war, with both Libyans and Nubians taking part. Five years later the priests, led by Herihor, took control from the pharaohs and, in 1070 BC, the New Kingdom came to an end with the death of Rameses XI.

◆ *Toys for Egyptian children included spinning tops, balls and wooden animals, some of which could be pulled along on wheels.*

INVASIONS

The country was once again divided. Herihor ruled the south from Thebes, and, in the north, a Libyan merchant called Smendes started the 21st dynasty, which had its capital at Tanis.

Nubian pharaohs followed the Libyan ones. They encouraged the study of the past and a return to the artistic standards of the Old Kingdom. During their rule all crafts, and especially metalwork, flourished.

The wealth of Egypt attracted other rulers, too, and in 671 BC the Assyrians invaded the country. With their new iron weapons, they won control over the Egyptians by 663 BC. But the Egyptians regained their independence seven years later, with the help of the Greeks.

In 525 BC, Egypt was invaded again, this time by the Persians. They ruled until 404 BC, when the Greeks helped once more to put an Egyptian pharaoh back on the throne.

The Persians returned in 343 BC. Then in 332 BC Alexander the Great conquered Egypt and added it to his large empire. He founded a new city in Lower Egypt and named it Alexandria.

After Alexander's death, a Greek family called the Ptolemies came to power. They ruled Egypt for almost 300 years.

◆ *Jewellery-making was a skilled craft. Workers in gold and semi-precious stones each had a special title.*

The Ptolemies spread Greek culture throughout Egypt during their reign. They established Alexandria as the country's capital, and built the world's first museum there, as well as the largest library in the world at that time. The last of the dynasty was Cleopatra VII, who came to the throne in 51 BC.

CLEOPATRA

Born in 69 BC, Cleopatra became co-ruler of Egypt with her half-brother, Ptolemy XII, when she was 18. She was famed for her charm and intelligence. The Roman leaders Julius Caesar and Mark Antony both fell in love with her.

She had a son with Julius Caesar, who helped her to regain her position after her brother ousted her from the throne in 48 BC. When Rome declared war on Egypt in 32 BC, Mark Antony led Cleopatra's forces. The Romans defeated the Egyptians and Mark Antony at the battle of Actium in 31 BC. A year after the defeat, both Mark Antony and Cleopatra committed suicide. Egypt then became a province of the Roman empire with a Roman governor.

♦ *The Nile remained an important trade route to the Mediterranean as well as to the rest of Africa. At towns along its banks, Egyptians traded grain for gold and jewels, ivory and even wild animals. Leopards and monkeys, for instance, were pets for the wealthy.*

♦ Many Egyptians had *shabti* figures buried with them when they died. They believed that the shabtis would come to life on a command from Osiris and perform tasks for the dead person. Sety I's shabti figure is inscribed with a pledge that it would carry out agricultural tasks for the pharaoh in the afterlife.

Shabti figure

♦ The Rosetta stone dates from 196 BC and is inscribed with a decree issued by Ptolemy V. The decree appears in hieroglyphs, in demotic (the popular language of the time) and in Greek.

When the stone was found in 1799, it enabled scholars to decipher hieroglyphs, which had puzzled them for years.

♦ Senet was a popular game, played with two sets of counters on a board with 30 squares. The winner was the first to take all his or her pieces off the board.

Senet board

THE FAR EAST

The ancient Chinese civilization is the best-known of the Far East. People started to settle and farm in the valley of the Huang He River around in 6000 BC. Villages developed along the river and also in the Hangzhou Bay area, where people grew rice from around 5000 BC.

By about 2700 BC the first leaders to rule over large areas began to emerge. Eventually they united the country under a series of dynasties. Under these rulers, cities such as Anyang, Xianyang and Chang'an developed.

Through the silk trade, the ancient Chinese had contact with many other civilizations in the Far East and beyond. Some, such as those of Japan and Korea, were greatly influenced by the Chinese. The Chinese, however, thought that their civilization was superior to everyone else's, and did not allow it to be influenced by any outsiders.

◆ *A palace building at Anyang, a Shang capital.*

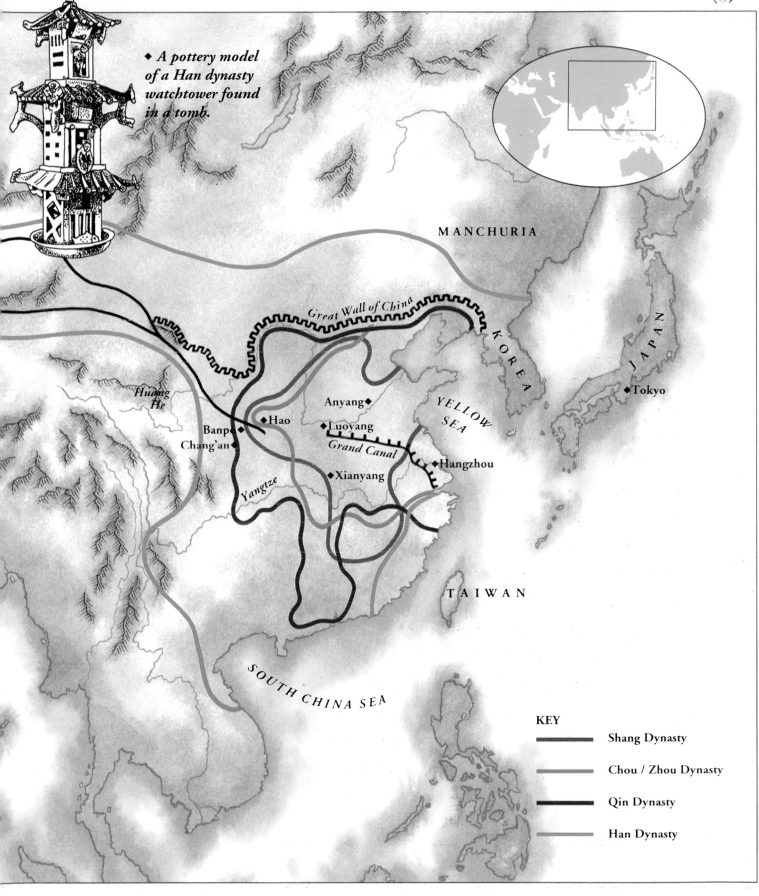

◆ *A pottery model of a Han dynasty watchtower found in a tomb.*

MANCHURIA

Great Wall of China

KOREA

JAPAN

◆Tokyo

Huang He

YELLOW SEA

Anyang ◆
◆Hao
Banpo◆   ◆Luoyang
Chang'an
Grand Canal
◆Hangzhou
◆Xianyang
Yangtze

TAIWAN

SOUTH CHINA SEA

KEY

———— Shang Dynasty

———— Chou / Zhou Dynasty

———— Qin Dynasty

———— Han Dynasty

THE FIRST CHINESE CIVILIZATIONS

CHINA TO 1122 BC

Early Chinese communities had grown up in the valley of the Huang He River by around 6000 BC. In villages such as Banpo, shown below, people kept chickens, dogs and pigs and grew crops. The fertile, yellowish soil in the area was quite loose, and easy to work with stone tools. The Banpo villagers planted millet, which thrived in the dry climate.

Other early Chinese peoples settled around the east coast, near Hangzhou Bay. Here the wet conditions were ideal for growing rice.

◆ Large pottery jars were used for storing water and grain, as well as for cooking. They could also be traded for other goods.

These first communities probably arose quite separately, without any idea that other groups existed.

An early people known as the Yangshao grew up in north China. They are famous for the beautiful painted clay pots they made.

In the east, the culture of the peoples called the Longshan lasted from around 3000 BC to 2400 BC. By the end of this time, the Chinese were starting to use bronze, instead of stone, to make their tools and weapons.

Farming was still the most important way of life, but society was beginning to change. Some people became wealthier and more powerful than others, and began to rule as kings.

THE SHANG DYNASTY

The first rulers were said to be the kings of the Xia dynasty (2100 BC–1726 BC), but there is no firm historical evidence to prove that they existed. The first dynasty we know about for certain was that of the Shang (1726 BC–1122 BC). Oracle bones recorded the

◆ Some of the houses in Banpo were built partly underground and had a fire pit in the centre for cooking and heating. The roofs of the houses were held up by wooden poles tied together and supported by wooden pillars inside.

◆ *In battle Shang soldiers wore heavy body armour, which was made mostly from bamboo and wood and padded with cloth.*

history of the Shang dynasty and give the names of all the rulers.

During this time, bronze casting became more and more important and communities of bronze casters developed. Other craftworkers were attracted to these communities, which then grew into towns and cities, such as Anyang, the Shang capital. Here they built houses, palaces, temples and tombs.

Most people still made a living by working on the land. The Shang kings claimed ownership of the land for themselves, but allowed other people to own land on their behalf. Farmers were then required to fight as soldiers for them when necessary.

The Shang also kept slaves in cruel conditions. Sometimes they were sacrificed to honour dead ancestors. Eventually, in 1122 BC, many slaves revolted and joined the Zhou army when it attacked Anyang and defeated the last of the Shang kings.

◆ *Archaeologists know that Banpo was a village of around 500 people. There was a large communal building in the middle of the village and a ditch around the outskirts.*

◆ Chinese writing was developed during the Shang dynasty. The earliest examples are found on oracle bones, used to read the future.

Oracle bone

◆ During this period, craftworkers made items for decoration and for practical purposes. Jade carvings were popular and were sometimes used in religious ceremonies.

Jade open ring

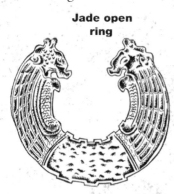

◆ Wealthy Chinese people had their clothes made from silk. It kept them cool in summer.

Silkworms on mulberry leaves

THE ZHOU DYNASTY: UPHEAVALS

1122–221 BC

The Zhou kings ruled China for just over 900 years. Because there were many upheavals during this time, the dynasty is split into the Western Zhou (1122–770 BC) and Eastern Zhou (770–221 BC). Eastern Zhou is divided into the Spring and Autumn period (770–476 BC) and the Warring States period (476–221 BC).

At first, the way of life under the Zhou rulers was less advanced than under the Shang, but soon Shang ways were adopted. Agriculture, writing and bronze casting continued. The feudal system was also kept, with society divided into nobles, peasants and slaves.

The capital was moved from Anyang to Hao, and the kings called themselves the Sons of Heaven. They thought that they were descended from a

◆ *The Chinese discovered how to make large bronze bells by making the parts separately and joining them together.*

god called the Millet Ruler and that heaven had given them permission to rule. They also believed that, if they ruled badly, heaven would remove its permission and they would be defeated.

SPRING AND AUTUMN PERIOD
In 770 BC, nomadic people from the north attacked

◆ *In times of upheaval, soldiers ruthlessly destroyed the enemy's crops.*

Confucius and Lao Tzu

The philosopher K'ung Fu-tzu or Confucius (551–479 BC), whose name means 'Great Master Kung', was born in the Zhou period. He taught that everyone had a place in society and that people had a responsibility towards one another.

Confucius

Lao Tzu, 'the Old Master', was another philosopher who attracted a large number of followers. He taught that people should lead a simple life in harmony with nature. It is thought that he wrote the *Tao Te Ching*, 'The Way of Life'. Lao Tzu's teachings are known as Taoism.

the Zhou kingdom, and defeated the king. He was replaced by King Ping, who moved the capital to Luoyang. This was the start of the Spring and Autumn period.

Iron now replaced bronze as a stronger and more widespread material for tools and weapons, and more crops were produced. Some nobles became richer and more powerful. They began to fight among themselves and in 476 BC war broke out.

THE WARRING STATES PERIOD

The Warring States period was a difficult time for the Chinese, with around 200 small states struggling for power. The rich people in states that were defeated lost their lands, while the poor everywhere were heavily taxed to pay soldiers. Men were conscripted into the army, so farms were short of labour. In 221 BC, the state of Qin became powerful enough to control the whole country.

◆ The Chinese belief that everything was in harmony with everything else was shown in the Yin and Yang symbol, with dark-coloured Yin interlocking with light-coloured Yang and each containing a small portion of the other.

Yin and Yang symbol

Chinese writing

◆ Chinese writing was made up of pictograms which represented words, or ideas, rather than sounds. By the time of the Zhou dynasty many thousands of them were in use and they were changing from simple pictures to complicated symbols which were less easy to recognize.

◆ Axes were used for battle and for ceremonies, as well as being useful tools. Ceremonial axes were often highly decorated.

Axehead

THE QIN DYNASTY: SHI HUANGDI

221–206 BC

The Qin (pronounced chin) dynasty governed China for only 15 years, but its first ruler, Shi Huangdi, was an energetic leader whose reforms had a lasting effect on the country.

Originally, Shi Huangdi was king of the western state of Qin. By 221 BC, he had conquered all the other states to turn China into an empire, with himself as emperor.

To unite the country after years of war, he reorganized the government and brought everything under his control. The peasants were made to pay taxes directly to him. He took power away from the noble families and forced them to live in Xianyang, his capital city, where he could watch over them and keep them away from their supporters.

The country was divided up into new administrative districts, to make it easier to govern. The canals were improved and new roads were built, so that the emperor's officials could travel quickly all over the land.

To make sure that his orders could be understood throughout the empire, Shi Huangdi ruled that the same system of writing should be used everywhere. The system of weights and measures, the coinage, and the distance between the wheels on a cart were made standard as well.

◆ Shi Huangdi was buried in a tomb with an army of over 7,500 life-size terracotta warriors, to guard him and the treasures he would need for the afterlife.

Shi Huangdi had the Great Wall built between 214 and 204 BC, to protect his empire from the peoples to the north. The wall stretched for 2,250 kilometres.

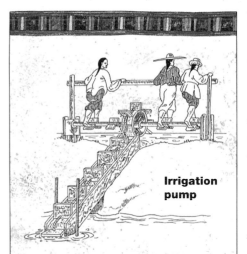

Irrigation pump

Early coinage

Different areas of China each had different coins: some round, some spade-shaped, some shaped like knives. These shapes probably came from times when goods were bartered and spades and knives were valuable items of trade. Shi Huangdi made everybody use round, bronze coins.

◆ Shi Huangdi improved the food supply in China by having irrigation systems built to carry water to the fields. Many small canals were dug and water was lifted from them into the fields, using pumps.

◆ Shi Huangdi was afraid of death. His palace contained over 1,000 bedrooms and he slept in a different room each night, to foil any assassination plot. He died of natural causes.

The emperor's chief adviser, Li Si, believed in an idea known as Legalism. This said that people were basically bad and so must be forced to obey the emperor's laws, or be put to death. This meant that Shi Huangdi's rule was often very brutal.

To stop people thinking back to the past, Shi Huangdi ordered the burning of all books which were not about the Qin dynasty and had over 400 scholars killed. He wanted to prevent people from following the teachings of Confucius and Lao Tzu. He forced many to work on his building projects, such as the Great Wall, the canals and the irrigation systems.

Shi Huangdi feared that the people would rebel, and he needed to know that the army could not be called out without his permission. He therefore had a system of tallies. The emperor kept one half of each tally, and the commanders of his army kept the other. Both parts of the tally had to be shown for the army to accept an order.

Shi Huangdi died in 210 BC and was followed by his son, who was harsh, weak and greedy. In 209 BC, the peasants rebelled. A large army was soon raised and in 206 BC the emperor was defeated and China split into a number of small states again.

Details from the terracotta army

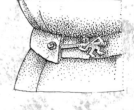

◆ The terracotta army included charioteers, foot soldiers and bowmen as well as officers, recognizable by their elaborate headgear. Great attention was paid to every detail, even belt buckles.

THE HAN DYNASTY: UNITING THE LAND

202 BC–AD 220

The Han dynasty gained control of China in 202 BC. Its rulers reunited the whole country and called themselves emperors. They tried to replace all the writings destroyed by Shi Huangdi during the Qin dynasty and allowed people to study the works of Confucius again.

To help him rule over such a vast area, each Han emperor had many government officials and civil servants. The officials made sure that everybody knew about the laws and obeyed them and that everybody paid the right amount of tax. The most important officials were called mandarins. To get their jobs they first had to pass examinations, based on the teachings of Confucius.

EXPANSION

The Han emperors were less harsh than the Qin had been and, under their rule, China started to flourish. The Emperor Wu Ti added a large part of central Asia to the empire, as well as southern Manchuria and much of the southeast coast of China. A census taken in AD 2 showed that there were 59,594,978 people living under Han rule.

Increasing trade within the empire and beyond brought wealth to the rapidly growing towns and cities such as Chang'an. This was the capital of Han China where the emperor and the noble families lived in luxury. More than two-thirds of the city was occupied by royal palaces, some of which had tall pavilions up to 115 metres high in their palace grounds.

◆ *Country people came to the city to buy or sell food and animals. In the noisy bustling streets, letter-writers, astrologers, barbers and dentists offered their services alongside craftworkers, farmers and traders.*

◆ *A bronze model of a rich man in his chariot. This model was found in the tomb of a Han official. It was made during the 2nd century AD. Later Chinese metalworkers started to use iron.*

At the same time, the Chinese moved ahead with scientific and technological discoveries and inventions. For example, they worked out that there are 365.25 days in a year; they discovered magnetic rocks called lodestones, which they used as compasses when siting their temples; they invented a breastplate harness, which made it easier for a horse to pull a heavy load; and they built bamboo bridges across some of the gorges in the Himalayas. Although iron was now used for tools and weapons, bronze casters continued to make fine models and ornaments. Some of the most graceful of them show galloping horses.

THE END OF THE DYNASTY
Eventually, the Han dynasty ran into problems. The population growth meant there was not enough land to go round. The peasants could not make enough money to buy food and pay taxes. The borders of the empire were attacked, and the Han army leaders seized control of the soldiers. In AD 220, the last Han emperor gave up his throne and the empire split again.

◆ *In 113 BC Prince Liu Cheng was buried in this suit made from over 2,000 wafer-thin pieces of jade, held together with gold, silver and bronze threads. It was thought that the jade would preserve the prince's body, but when the tomb was excavated in 1968 the body had crumbled.*

Acupuncture chart

◆ By Han times, the Chinese were using acupuncture to treat illnesses. Charts showed where the tips of needles should be inserted into the body to cure different problems.

◆ Paper-making was a Han invention. At first, paper was made from silk fibres, but later on, plants and rags were used. Paper documents soon became fairly common.

◆ A court astronomer invented the seismograph. When an earthquake made the bronze vase shake, one of the dragon's mouths opened, dropping a ball into the mouth of the toad below.

Seismograph

A TIME OF CHAOS: A DIVIDED LAND

AD 220–618

China now split into Wei in the north, Shu in the west and Wu in the south and east. This period in Chinese history is called the Three Kingdoms. Life was hard, especially in the north which was always under threat of invasion by nomads.

For a period from AD 265 until 317, China was reunited under the Western Chin. Then the nomads began a more successful invasion from the north and advanced as far as the Yangtze River before they were defeated. The Eastern Chin then took control of southern China, but the north was divided up again into many small states.

The country stayed united in culture. The invaders settled and followed Chinese ways, and the culture of people who had fled south became incorporated into the southern way of life.

Nevertheless, the upheavals made China much poorer. Farmers could hardly grow enough food to feed everybody. People had to pay high taxes and were forced to be soldiers in the army for long periods of time.

◆ *Yang Di forced people to work on the building of his palaces and pleasure parks. To cover the costs of these vast building schemes, he increased taxes and asked for ten years' payment in advance.*

The Grand Canal linked the Huang He and Yangtze Rivers, making it easier to travel north and south as well as east and west in China. The canal was always busy and many people lived on it permanently.

In 581, Yang Chien seized power in northern China, and his army then conquered the south. He reunited China under the Sui dynasty, made his capital at Chang'an and ruled firmly from there. He reduced taxes and the amount of time that people had to spend in the army.

YANG DI

Yang Chien was succeeded by his son, Yang Di, who also tried to improve China. He spent vast amounts of money on rebuilding the Grand Canal, which linked the rice fields along the Yangtze River to the cities of Chang'an and Luoyang. When it opened,

it is said that 80,000 labourers were needed to tow the boats for him, his family and his officials. In AD 607 he forced over one million men to work on the task of repairing the Great Wall. They had to work for 20 days, and many of them died. Eventually the peasants rebelled, Yang Di was killed and the Sui dynasty collapsed.

Merchants travelling along the Silk Road brought Buddhism from India to China. By the end of the Sui dynasty Buddhism had spread across the empire and many shrines, temples and monasteries had been built.

◆ The Chinese invented the wheelbarrow, although at first they used it to carry people around, rather than heavy loads.

Wheelbarrow

◆ Sometimes the rivers in China caused floods which washed away crops and even whole villages. At other times, there was not enough water. Yang Chien set up irrigation schemes to control the flow of water and enable farmers to grow more.

Pottery figure of a rider wearing stirrups

◆ Another Chinese invention from this time was the stirrup. Stirrups made horse riding safer. They also left the rider's hands free for using weapons in a battle.

THE EARLY PEOPLES OF JAPAN

16,000 BC–AD 500

The Japanese islands are thought to have split away from the mainland of Asia in about 18,000 BC. Archaeologists have found finely crafted stone tools of that time.

By 16,000 BC people were making pottery vessels from coils of clay and using cords to decorate them. Known as Jomon pottery, from the Japanese word for 'cord-marked', they gave their name to a period of Japanese history which lasted until around 500 BC.

The population of Japan expanded in this period. Most people led a settled life. Unlike people in other parts of the world, they did not start farming, because game and fish were plentiful.

By 300 BC, however, rice and barley were being grown on the Japanese islands. A new way of life began, with people living in villages ruled by a chief. Bronze and iron began to be used for tools, weapons and ceremonial goods. These metals were probably brought across from south Korea.

This new culture is called the Yayoi. It is named after the site in present-day Tokyo where archaeologists found evidence of the civilization.

◆ *The Ainu, or Ezo, were the original inhabitants of Japan, living there long before those who moved over from the Asian mainland. Some people of Ainu descent still live in northern Japan today.*

◆ *The Shinto religion has its roots in the Japanese Bronze Age and its name means 'way of the* kami *(gods)'. These* kami *are found in nature and in the spirits of the dead. At ceremonies in temples like this one, the* kami *were asked to send good harvests, good health and many children.*

◆ *Small clay models of servants, scribes, soldiers, animals and everyday objects were placed in and around the tombs of the wealthy Japanese. Some tombs also had scenes painted inside.*

In about AD 167, an elderly priestess called Himiko united 30 small Japanese states under her rule. Himiko sent ambassadors to China, which was flourishing under the Han dynasty, to seek friendship and advice. Chinese influence in Japan was strong from then on.

THE YAMATO PERIOD

The Yamato people came from the central plain of Japan's main island. What is called the Yamato period in Japan lasted from around AD 200 to 646.

Shinto Ritual

Purity and cleanliness were important in Shinto religion, for they were thought to help keep society in order. Before going into a shrine, people washed their mouths out with special cleansing water.

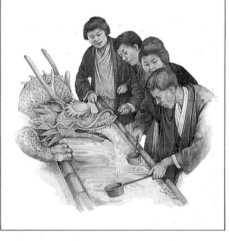

During the 3rd and 4th centuries AD, the Yamato gained control of most of central Japan. To reinforce their authority over the people they had conquered, they claimed to be descended from the Japanese Sun goddess, Amaterasu. Right until the present day, Japanese emperors can trace their family line back to the Yamato.

In the 5th century AD, the Japanese conquered parts of southern Korea and became rich on the tribute which they forced Korean kings to pay. By the end of the 5th century, the Koreans started to reclaim their lands and the tribute was no longer paid.

◆ In Jomon times, villages developed by rivers, lakes and the sea. The thatched houses were built over shallow pits, to give extra protection from winter cold and summer heat.

Jomon thatched house

◆ In the Yayoi period, some bodies were placed inside stone coffins for burial, but others were placed inside pottery double jars. The largest of these measures two metres in height. The burial sites were sometimes marked with stones.

Burial jars

◆ After Japan separated from mainland Asia, the Japanese used wooden boats to continue trade and other contacts with Korea.

Model boat found in a 6th-century tomb

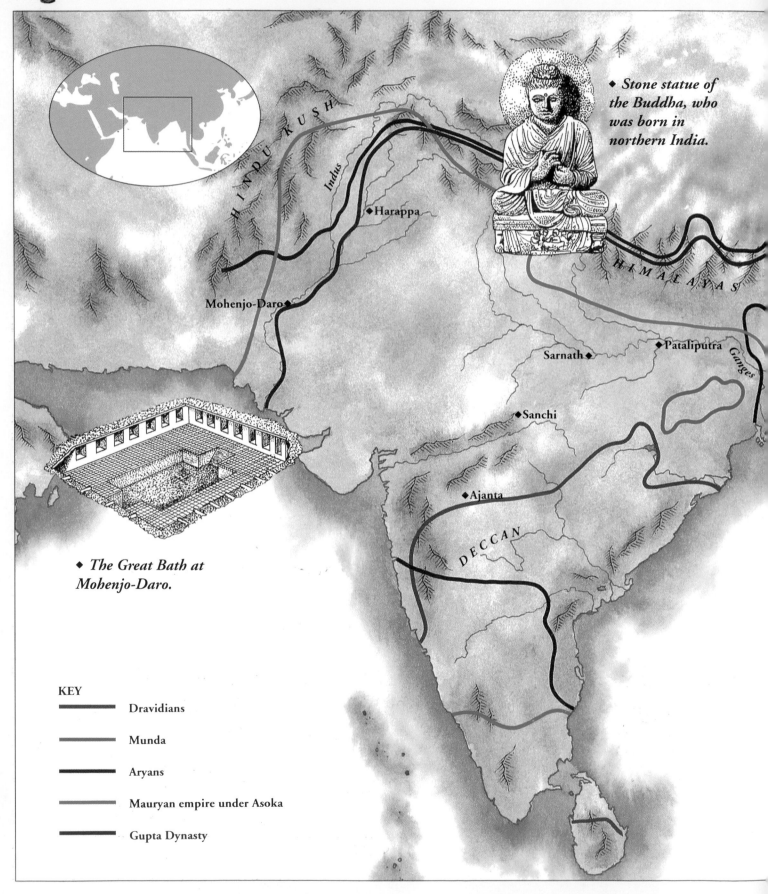

◆ *Stone statue of the Buddha, who was born in northern India.*

Harappa

Mohenjo-Daro◆

Sarnath ◆

◆ Pataliputra

◆ Sanchi

◆Ajanta

HINDU KUSH

Indus

HIMALAYAS

Ganges

DECCAN

◆ *The Great Bath at Mohenjo-Daro.*

KEY

—— Dravidians

—— Munda

—— Aryans

—— Mauryan empire under Asoka

—— Gupta Dynasty

THE INDUS VALLEY AND INDIA

The first attempts at farming in the Indian subcontinent were in the hills west of the Indus Valley around 6500 BC. Shortly after, rice was grown in the wetter Ganges Valley.

In the Indus Valley, where the river deposited silt over the land in its annual flood, so many crops were grown that by 2500 BC cities such as Mohenjo-Daro could be built.

The Himalayas form a natural barrier in the northeast, so invaders, as well as new ideas, came from the northwest. Around 1500 BC these invaders included the Aryans.

Despite the barriers, there were trade links with the Chinese and Roman empires and the Spice Islands of Indo-China. The Mauryan capital of Pataliputra was influenced by the Persians, while India itself influenced other cultures through the spread of Buddhism.

◆ *Buddhist pilgrims in the 2nd century AD in India.*

MOHENJO-DARO AND HARAPPA

2500–1500 BC

By 2500 BC the people of the Indus Valley had started to build towns. The largest were Mohenjo-Daro and Harappa but about a hundred more are known.

Both Mohenjo-Daro and Harappa had planned streets, with workmen's barracks, large public buildings and granaries all made out of bricks baked in wood-fired ovens. The houses were brick-built, too, and most of them had several rooms, a courtyard, a well and a lavatory. At the centre of each town was an artificial mound, which acted as a citadel.

In Mohenjo-Daro the remains of a building known as the Great Bath have also been excavated. The bath itself was 12 metres long and 3 metres deep and was lined with a tar-like substance to make it waterproof. Wooden steps led into the water at the two narrow ends and a well probably provided the water.

We know nothing about religious beliefs in the Indus Valley at this time, but it seems likely that the Great Bath was used for ritual bathing, rather than for swimming for pleasure.

◆ *Transport over land was by ox-drawn cart. This must have been very slow, so the river was probably used for transport between the cities.*

INDUS VALLEY LIFE

The economy of the Indus Valley depended on trade and agriculture, and the main crops grown were barley, wheat, melons and dates. Animals in the area included elephants, water buffalo and rhinoceroses.

The Indus Valley people were the first to make cloth from cotton. Potters used the wheel to

◆ *Both Mohenjo-Daro and Harappa covered about 60 hectares of land and housed around 40,000 people. They both had shops. Excavations in the ruins of the cities have revealed that almost every house was connected to sewers and a water supply.*

make pots. Most tools were made from stone, although knives, bowls, figures and also weapons were made from bronze. The weapons were probably for hunting rather than for warfare.

The cities had a standard system of weights and measures. There was also a writing system which used pictograms. No one in modern times has been able to translate these.

As well as links between the cities, there were trade links by land with Badakhstan and Persia, and by sea with the Persian Gulf and Mesopotamia.

Much about life in the Indus Valley is not known. For example, we do not know how society was structured, or whether people were ruled by a king or an

♦ *Archaeologists began to excavate the site of Mohenjo-Daro in the 1920s. The mound shown above was the stronghold of the town.*

assembly. There are no ruins of a palace where rulers might once have lived.

The Indus Valley civilization flourished until about 1500 BC when it suddenly ended. No one is certain why. It might have been because the Indus River changed its course, making it impossible to grow enough crops, or because the people could no longer resist attacks by the Aryans from the northwest.

♦ *Indus Valley pictograms appear on this seal. More than 1,200 seals have been found at Mohenjo-Daro. The animal may be a sacred bull.*

♦ In the courtyards of many houses in Mohenjo-Daro, brick-lined shafts have been found. They were possibly wells, but could also have been used for storing a supply of grain or cooking oil.

Brick-lined shaft

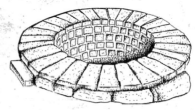

♦ Bead workshops in the Indus Valley produced necklaces made from gold, tin, glazed earthenware, soapstone and cornelians.

Beads from Mohenjo-Daro

♦ Although the Indus Valley civilization disappeared completely, pottery figures excavated from some sites are very similar to those produced in India 1,500 years later.

Mother-goddess figure

ARYAN INDIA: TRIBAL TIMES

1500–400 BC

The Aryans were nomadic herders who left their homeland in the steppes of southern Russia around 1800 BC and migrated southwestwards. They passed through Anatolia, Persia and the Hindu Kush and arrived in the Indus Valley at about the time the civilization there collapsed.

◆ *Although the people in the Aryan villages farmed as individual families and not as communities, everyone worked together at busy times such as this, when the rice seedlings were planted in the flooded fields by the Ganges River.*

Once in the Indus Valley, the Aryans began to settle in tribal villages. Their houses were made from bamboo and clay. At first, they counted their wealth in cattle and sheep and often raided other people's herds. Gradually, they spread as far as the Ganges Valley and started to plough the land and grow wheat and rice as well as keep animals. The Aryans had come from a harsh climate and so they were physically tougher than the earlier people of this area had been. They enjoyed fighting, chariot racing and gambling, as well as eating plenty of meat and drinking wine.

They divided their society into four classes, with the Brahmans, or priests, at the top. Then came the Kshatriyas (nobles and soldiers), followed by the Vaisyas (farmers and traders). At the bottom were the Shudras, whose job was to serve the other three classes. Even lower than the Shudras were the non-Aryan people whose lands had been dominated by the invaders.

THE *VEDAS*

The Aryans' language, Sanskrit, was only spoken, not written, so their history

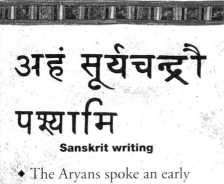

अहं सूर्यचन्द्रौ पश्यामि
Sanskrit writing

◆ The Aryans spoke an early form of Sanskrit which is the basis of languages spoken in northern India today. The writing above means 'I see the Sun and the Moon'. The word *arya* in Sanskrit means 'noble', which shows the influence the Aryans had on India.

◆ The Aryans used the chariot in war, as well as for travelling and for entertainment in races.

The Aryan god Indra

◆ Indra was the Aryans' most important god. He was the god of war and storms and the creator of the universe. In later times he was replaced by Vishnu, Shiva and Krishna.

and beliefs were passed down by word of mouth. The *Vedas,* or Books of Knowledge, were written down much later. They are the basis of the Hindu religion, but they also tell us much about life in Aryan times. From around 1000 BC, Aryan farmers used iron tools which made it possible to clear more trees and plough more of the heavier soils of the Ganges Valley. They also set up irrigation schemes. They were then able to grow more crops, which could support larger towns.

By 600 BC there were 16 major Aryan kingdoms in northern India, each with towns protected by great ramparts of mud bricks. We know their names from two epic poems called the *Mahabharata* and the *Ramayana* which were written down around AD 1300.

◆ *The Hindu Kush is a mountain range in central Asia. It is about 800 kilometres in length and its highest peak is 7,692 metres high.*

◆ *An illustration from a book of the epic Hindu poem, the* Mahabharata. *This story has its roots in Aryan India, but was written down much later.*

THE MAURYAN EMPIRE AND GUPTA DYNASTY

321 BC–AD 467

◆ *Parts of India are hot and dusty and so Asoka ordered that groves of banyan trees should be planted alongside roads, to provide shade for weary travellers.*

The Indus Valley became part of the Persian empire in the late 6th century BC, and the name India was first used. When Alexander the Great conquered the Persians, India became part of his empire briefly, until Chandragupta Maurya seized power in 321 BC and founded the Mauryan empire. Stretching from Bengal to the Hindu Kush, it united the lands of northern India, including the Aryan states.

The empire reached its peak under Chandragupta's grandson, Asoka, who came to power in 273 BC. He spent 11 years enlarging his empire by conquering neighbouring states. Then, after one horrific battle, he became a Buddhist and stopped going to war.

To try to unite the many different peoples in his empire, Asoka promoted a set of beliefs which included religious tolerance, non-violence and respect for other people. He still employed a secret police force to help him run his empire, but also tried to improve living conditions, saying 'All men are my children'.

He encouraged the spread of Buddhism throughout his empire.

When he died, in 232 BC, the Mauryan empire began to break up. In 185 BC it collapsed and India split up into separate states.

GUPTA DYNASTY

The Guptas came to power in AD 320. They came from the kingdom of Magadha in the Ganges Valley and ruled most of India for around 150 years. In that time, trade by land and sea increased. Silks and spices, gold and jewels came into the country. Some were traded again for other goods from as far away as the Roman empire. New Hindu villages were established on land which had not been cultivated

◆ *Asoka had his wishes carved on stones, pillars and rocks, which can still be found throughout India today.*

Buddhism remained popular and many statues of the Buddha were set up. Music, dance, art and literature flourished and Kalidasa, India's most celebrated dramatist and poet, was writing about the beauty of nature, love and adventure at this time. Other entertainments included magic, acrobatics and wrestling.

New customs developed during Gupta times. These included the Hindu practice of *suttee*, in which the widow was burned to death on her husband's funeral pyre. Another custom introduced was child marriage, in which young children became engaged to one another and young girls could be married off to much older men.

before, and Hindu priests played an important part in their development as they were knowledgeable about farming. The villagers also believed that the priests could protect them from evil. Cities began to develop on the Deccan plateau in central India and trade flourished there too, both over land and by sea.

♦ *Wall paintings from the caves at Ajanta show musicians and dancers entertaining the royal family.*

♦ This lion capital topped one of Asoka's columns at Sarnath, where the Buddha preached. A fourth lion faces the back. Modern India has adopted this capital as one of its symbols.

Lion capital at Sarnath

♦ To improve people's living conditions, Asoka built hospitals and rest-houses and set up irrigation schemes.

Asoka

♦ Elephants were used successfully in warfare. One Macedonian general gave Chandragupta vast areas of land west of the Indus in exchange for 500 elephants for his army.

Elephant seal

HINDUISM AND BUDDHISM

1000 BC–AD 500

Two major world religions developed in India. The earlier of them was Hinduism, one of the oldest living faiths in the world. It evolved over many hundreds of years, stretching back to pre-historic times, and is the religion of 83 percent of Indians now.

Hindu beliefs have much in common with the beliefs of the Aryans, including the division of society into groups or castes. For Hindus, the supreme power in the universe is Brahman. Three aspects of Brahman are expressed in the form of the gods Brahma, Vishnu and Shiva, and these three have many forms or incarnations. The different god images helped people understand the idea of Brahman.

◆ Both Hindus and Buddhists believe that life is an endless cycle of birth and death. They believe that there is a life after death and that people are reincarnated many times, depending on how they have lived their previous life. The Wheel of Life used in Buddhist temples is a symbol of this.

◆ After the Buddha died, his remains were buried in mounds called stupas. King Asoka redivided the relics and built new stupas to hold them all over India. The Great Stupa at Sanchi is one of the biggest.

BUDDHISM

Buddhism was founded by Siddhartha Gautama, who came to be called the Buddha, which means 'enlightened one'. He was a wealthy prince who lived in northern India around 2,500 years ago, from about 563 BC to about 485 BC.

The Buddha led a quiet, sheltered life until the age of 29. He then encountered old age, sickness and death for the first time. This worried him so much that he left his palace to search for the cause of and cure for suffering. Through meditation he found an answer to his questions. He said that it was possible to reach a state of eternal peace, called 'Nirvana'. He soon had many followers.

The Buddha's disciples spread the word throughout India and the new religion went some way towards becoming the main Indian belief. Hinduism, however, was too strong. By the beginning of the 3rd century AD, Buddhism had declined in India, although it spread throughout other eastern countries.

Despite their differences, Hinduism and Buddhism have much in common, including a belief in reincarnation and in the need for truth, non-violence and respect for other living creatures.

◆ *The Hindu caste system divided society into four groups with similar names to those used by the Aryans. At the top were the Brahmans or priests. They were followed by the Kshatriyas or warriors and the Vaisyas or merchants, and below them were the Suhdras or serfs. People who did not fit in any group were outcastes or untouchables.*

◆ As Buddhism spread through India, places that the Buddha was said to have visited were sometimes decorated with carvings of a footprint.

Buddhist footprint

◆ Krishna is one of the ten incarnations of Vishnu, the preserver. Vishnu is believed to appear when there is danger on Earth or when people need comforting.

Krishna

◆ The Sanskrit word OM is made up of three sounds: A, U and M. They can represent the three scriptures, the three incarnations of Brahman, or any other aspect of the Hindu religion consisting of three separate things.

'Om' symbol

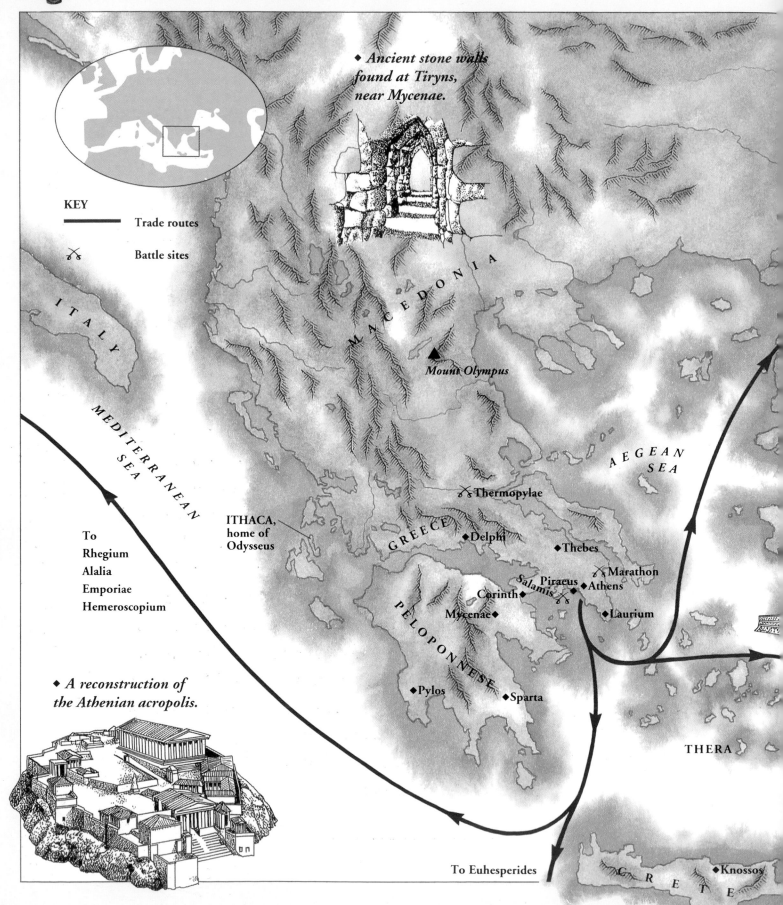

KEY

—————— Trade routes

⚔ Battle sites

◆ *Ancient stone walls found at Tiryns, near Mycenae.*

ITALY

MEDITERRANEAN SEA

To
Rhegium
Alalia
Emporiae
Hemeroscopium

MACEDONIA

▲ *Mount Olympus*

AEGEAN SEA

⚔ Thermopylae

GREECE

ITHACA,
home of
Odysseus

◆ Delphi

◆ Thebes

⚔ Marathon

Salamis Piraeus
◆ Corinth ◆ Athens
⚔
PELOPONNESE
◆ Mycenae   ◆ Laurium

◆ Pylos   ◆ Sparta

THERA

◆ *A reconstruction of the Athenian acropolis.*

To Euhesperides

CRETE ◆ Knossos

To Olbia

BLACK SEA

To Dioscurias

THRACE

Byzantium ◆

Troy

ANATOLIA

◆ *The Colossus at Rhodes, one of the seven wonders of the ancient world.*

LYDIA

IONIA

To Sidon

RHODES

THE AEGEAN CIVILIZATIONS

The geography of mainland Greece and the islands in the Aegean Sea had a great effect on the way civilizations developed there.

For example, because the mainland of Greece was near the Fertile Crescent, it was one of the first areas in Europe to farm. Some families became more powerful than others and began to take control of an area. The mountainous country, however, made it impossible for any one family to take control of the whole area, and this situation did not change until 146 BC when Greece became part of the Roman empire.

The history of civilization in the Aegean can be divided into five main periods: the time of the Minoans on Crete; that of the Mycenaeans; the Dark Ages; the Archaic period, in which the city-states such as Athens and Sparta developed; and the Classical period.

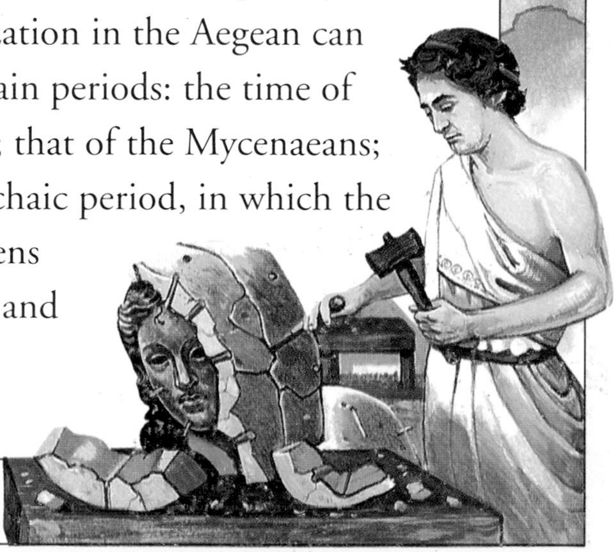

ANCIENT CRETE: THE MINOANS

2500–1450 BC

The Minoans are named after Minos, a famous king of Crete, although no one knows if or when he existed. According to legend, he ruled the Aegean Sea, and built a labyrinth on Crete in which he kept the minotaur, a monster that was half-bull, half-man.

The Minoan people lived on Crete, and other islands in the Aegean, from around 2500 BC. Their civilization was at its peak between 2200 BC and 1450 BC. During this time, several towns were built, each one centred on a palace.

Although they built palaces, the Minoans did not build temples. They worshipped their gods in sacred caves and at hilltop sanctuaries. They also had shrines in their homes. These were dedicated to the snake goddess, who was thought to be the guardian spirit of the home.

The Minoans were efficient farmers, and there was plenty of food to feed the population. This meant that not everybody needed to grow their own food, and so workers could develop other skills.

Minoan craftworkers were skilled potters and metalworkers, and carved beautiful objects from ivory and gemstones. Many of these artefacts have been found throughout the Aegean and in countries in the eastern Mediterranean, including Egypt. Clearly, the Minoans traded widely by sea, and owed much of their prosperity to trade.

THE PALACE AT KNOSSOS

Only a hundred years ago, archaeologists discovered the remains of a palace at Knossos, in the north of Crete. The palace had over one thousand rooms, including apartments for the king and queen, workshops and a school, with storerooms for the

◆ *Townspeople lived in houses which were usually two storeys high, with the living quarters upstairs and a storeroom at street level.*

The Minoan goldsmiths were highly skilled. This pendant is a reminder of the legend of the minotaur – the half-bull, half-man who was said to be kept in a labyrinth on the island.

THE END OF MINOAN CIVILIZATION

In spite of its wealth and organization, Minoan civilization came to an end in 1450 BC. There are several possible reasons why this happened. Agriculture in the east of the island suffered serious damage under volcanic ash from an eruption on the nearby island of Thera. Many of the harbours on which Minoan trade depended were damaged in the huge tidal wave which followed this eruption. Within a century the Minoans had lost their supremacy in the Aegean and the Mycenaeans based on the mainland were ready to take their place.

surplus grain, olive oil and wine. The walls of the palace were decorated with frescoes, depicting rituals at court and entertainments such as boxing and bull-leaping, in which an acrobat turned a somersault on the back of a bull. Clay tablets have written details relating to the way the palace was organized. One shows that in the 15th century BC as many as 4,300 people might have received food from the palace storerooms. Other tablets record that the palace controlled up to 80,000 sheep whose wool was spun and woven into cloth.

Wealthy Minoan women wore flounced skirts made up of many different pieces of material, and a bodice which laced at the waist. Wealthy men wore loincloths with wide belts, and elaborate headdresses, trimmed with feathers.

Clay tablet showing Linear A

Minoan writing developed from pictograms to a script called Linear A. This was followed by another script called Linear B, which was finally deciphered in 1952, when it was recognized as an early form of Greek. Linear A, however, remains a mystery.

Double axehead

The double axe-head, or labrys, was the symbol of the Minoans' mother-goddess. It was painted in a repetitive design throughout the palace at Knossos.

The palace at Knossos was built of stone and timber. Galleries overlooked a central courtyard. The private royal rooms were on the first floor with the public rooms above.

Reconstructed palace of Knossos

THE MYCENAEAN CIVILIZATION

1650–1100 BC

Mainland Greece is mountainous, and many separate states or kingdoms developed there. Because the state of Mycenae was the most powerful, it has given its name to the whole of the Bronze Age civilization, which began in Greece in around 1650 BC.

The Mycenaean civilization began as a series of small hilltop villages, many of which grew eventually into wealthy fortified towns. At first the Mycenaeans were greatly influenced by the Minoans, but after 1450 BC the situation turned around, and the Mycenaeans extended their own influence and political control to Crete.

PALACES

Unlike the Minoans, the Mycenaeans were warriors as well as farmers, traders and seafarers. Their palaces were well defended, at first with strong fences of pointed wooden stakes set close together, and later on with thick walls made of massive stone blocks. Inside the palaces, the rooms were arranged around courtyards and the walls and floors were plastered and painted with everyday scenes.

The palaces were the centre of political control. Mycenaean leaders ruled over huge areas of land, as well as overseeing trade and some industries.

Each palace had at least one cemetery, in which the rulers were buried in massive beehive-shaped tombs, known as *tholoi*. One tomb measures nearly 15 metres across. Gold and other precious objects have been found in the tombs, revealing the great wealth of the Mycenaean royal families and aristocracy.

• *The Lion Gate, the main entrance to Mycenae, was built in around 1300 BC. The city's defenders could attack their enemies from the two projecting walls. In spite of their strength, the walls did not protect Mycenae from destruction.*

Beyond the palace walls lay the town, in which craftworkers, traders and farmers lived. Crops such as wheat, barley, grapes and olives were grown on hillside terraces. Most of the grain went to the palace granary, while the grapes and olives were pressed to make wine and oil.

Any produce that was not needed for the local people was taken by traders to southern Italy and Sicily, and throughout the eastern Mediterranean. In exchange, they got copper from Cyprus and Sardinia, ivory from Syria, tin from Anatolia and gold and alabaster from Egypt.

Some of the Mycenaeans' wealth came from warfare. Bronze body-armour has been found in some tombs, and frescoes show that foot soldiers wore helmets and carried spears and shields.

◆ *Pylos was an important site of the Mycenaean civilization. The remains of the palace of King Nestor show that it was built around a series of courts, and its floors and walls were plastered.*

THE TROJAN WAR

The story of the war between Greece and Troy dates from this period. The legend may have its roots in a raid the Mycenaeans carried out on Troy in the late 1200s BC. The Greek leader, Agamemnon, was almost certainly a Mycenaean king.

In around 1250 BC the Mycenaeans built even more substantial defences around their palaces, because of the threat of attack. Fifty years later, most of their palaces were destroyed or abandoned, although we do not know who the attackers were. By 1100 BC the Mycenaean civilization had vanished.

◆ A gold funerary mask was found in a grave at Mycenae in the 1870s by Heinrich Schliemann, a German archaeologist. It was thought to be that of King Agamemnon, but today people think it is 300 years older.

Gold funerary mask

◆ Many of the paintings in Mycenaean palaces show hunting scenes. Nobles hunted wild boars using spears and shields. The dead animal's tusks were sliced lengthways and attached to a cloth cap, to make a warrior's helmet. It took several kills to get enough tusks to make a helmet.

◆ Excavations at the site of Troy have revealed nine cities built one on top of the other. The seventh one dates from the time of the legendary siege of Troy and there is evidence that it came to a violent end.

Ruins at Troy, in Turkey

FROM THE DARK AGES TO THE CITY-STATES

1100–500 BC

There are no written records of what happened in Greece following the collapse of the Mycenaean civilization. The next 500 years are known as the Dark Ages.

We know that the mainland was invaded by people from the north, including the Dorians. They spoke a form of Greek, but had no written language. In spite of this, they kept alive the memory of the Mycenaeans through the tradition of telling long narrative poems.

Stories of the Trojan War and of Mycenaean heroes eventually became Homer's epic poems, the *Iliad* and the *Odyssey*.

Many of the original inhabitants of the mainland moved out to the islands south and west of Greece, but the invaders gradually moved there too. Others moved east, to settle on the coast of Ionia or on the nearby islands. Here they continued farming and trading with their neighbours.

GROWTH OF THE CITY-STATES

During the Dark Ages, the Mycenaean towns fell into decay and were abandoned, but many villages survived. By 800 BC more had been created by newly settled populations. As these villages grew, they set up links with one another, and gradually one in each area became more important than the rest.

From these came the city-states, each consisting of a large town or city, known as the *polis,* plus its surrounding farmland and villages. The mountains around the cities provided them with a natural defence. In addition, the Greeks built high defensive walls around their cities. A fort called an *acropolis* was built at a high point within the walls. In time, this became the religious centre of each city-state, while an open space called the *agora* was the centre of political life.

◆ *The Athenians went to war in ships known as triremes. A hefty wooden pole, or ram, was fixed to the front. The ships were rowed at full speed into enemy ships in the hope that the ram would hole and sink them.*

◆ *Spartan soldiers, known as hoplites, wore armour and carried shields and spears. They fought in a close formation known as a phalanx, with shields overlapping so that each soldier was really protecting the next from attack.*

Although Athens and Sparta joined forces against the invading Persians at the battles of Marathon, Thermopylae and Salamis, from 431 to 404 BC they also fought against each other in the Peloponnesian War. Sparta won.

The mountainous landscape made communication between the city-states difficult. Each had its own laws, currency, government and army. Rivalry and even warfare were common between the city-states. This was especially true between Athens and Sparta.

◆ *The acropolis was the centre of each city-state. The temples erected on it were simple at first, but later more elaborate buildings such as the Parthenon in Athens were built.*

◆ Athena was the goddess of Athens and was portrayed as both a warrior and a judge. Her symbol, the owl, represented wisdom. It is shown on this four-drachma silver coin.

Greek coin

Greek alphabet

ΑΒΓΔΕϜΓ
ΔΙ
Ι ΚΛΜΝΟΓ
ϘΡΣ
ΤΥΤΤΧΥΖ

◆ The Greek alphabet developed during this period. Based on that used by the Phoenicians, it had symbols for vowels as well as for consonants.

◆ Spartan women were brought up to be strong. They were the mothers of some of the best warriors in Greece. This vase shows a softer side to Spartan women: a mother weeping as her son goes off to war.

Painted Greek vase

THE GOLDEN AGE OF GREECE

500–350 BC

By 500 BC the city-states were firmly established and, in spite of rivalry and occasional warfare between them, life for most people was very good. This period of Greek history is often known as the Classical period.

Crafts, trade and agriculture flourished, bringing in more wealth, and this made it possible for education, literature, architecture, mathematics, science and philosophy to develop more fully.

Life was probably not so good for slaves. They did the heavy or dirty work, or looked after the households of the wealthy, who were therefore free to follow politics or business matters.

Wealthy people helped to finance some of the fine public buildings which were erected during this period. These included open-air theatres where music and plays were performed and poetry was recited. Each city-state also had at least one gymnasium, where the Greeks could pursue their ideal of physical fitness.

Law courts and council chambers where

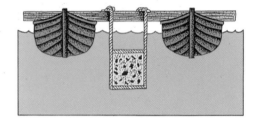

◆ *The Greeks needed vast quarries to supply stone for their buildings. Each quarry must have employed hundreds of people, as all the stone had to be cut by hand. Large blocks of stone were slung between two ships for transport by water.*

◆ *Bronze statues were made by pouring the molten metal into a clay mould. When the metal had hardened, the mould was broken to get the statue out.*

Corinthian

Ionic

Doric

◆ *Classical Greek temples had a colonnade of fluted columns around the outside, with one of three styles of column. Inside was the sanctuary containing a statue of the temple's god or goddess.*

public affairs could be discussed and controlled were probably built by the city-state. But the wealthy certainly helped to pay for some of the many new classical-style temples built at the time.

TEMPLES, GODS AND GODDESSES

The most important temples were on the acropolis in the centre of each city-state. As well as a temple to the local god or goddess, there would be others to popular deities such as Apollo, Zeus, Poseidon and Artemis. The gods were thought to live on Mount Olympus, which was a national shrine, as was the Oracle in the temple of Apollo at Delphi. The Greeks went there to try to find out what the future held.

Many of these buildings were made from marble and decorated with carved pictures of deities or past heroes. There were also lifelike statues made from marble or bronze.

The Athenians exploited the silver mines at Laurium to get metal to make coins. They needed them to pay for new buildings and to pay for regular festivals in the city. Many coins were also minted to finance the defence of the city and its port of Piraeus. Mercenaries were recruited to fight in the army, and fortifications known as the Long Walls were built between Athens and Piraeus to make sure the city could not be cut off from its port.

◆ The ancient Greek Olympic games included an event called the Pentathlon, which involved discus throwing, long jumping, javelin throwing, wrestling and sprinting.

Statue of discus thrower

◆ Life in Sparta was much tougher than it was in the other city-states. The Spartans had been frightened by a revolt of their slaves in 640 BC and so built up a powerful army to control them. To make sure that the strongest survived, weak babies were left on a mountain to die. Boys left home aged seven to train to be soldiers. They joined the army when they were 20 and, even if they married, they had to eat and sleep in the army barracks.

◆ This machine stood in a Greek temple. When a coin was dropped in the top, it triggered the mechanism to release a measured amount of holy water into the container.

Coin-operated machine, selling holy water

Ordinary homes were quite small and built around courtyards. Water came from wells or collected rainwater and there was no adequate sewage, refuse or drainage system. The narrow, unpaved streets were often muddy or dirty and a breeding ground for disease. Greek doctors studied human bodies carefully and tried to treat illnesses with medicines made from herbs and plants, instead of using charms and sacrifices. They built up records of what they used and recorded the results.

DISCOVERIES

Doctors and scholars used observation and reasoning to try to find out why things happened and how things worked. The physician Hippocrates correctly identified many illnesses, while mathematicians such as Euclid and Pythagoras discovered important rules of arithmetic and geometry.

Herodotus is regarded as having written the first true history book, about the wars between Greeks and Persians. Thucydides later wrote the first detailed account of a war and its causes when he described the Peloponnesian War in which he had served as a general.

Playwrights produced both comedies and tragedies, while philosophers such as Socrates, Plato and Aristotle made studies of life and its meaning which are still valued today.

What made the city-states so different from earlier societies was that all the men who were citizens of the state had a say in making its laws and could vote for the politicians of their choice in regular elections. Similarly, if political unrest threatened, the citizens could vote for a public

---

◆ *Going to the theatre in the open air was very popular, in spite of the hard stone seats. All the parts were played by men, who wore character masks as well as costumes.*

◆ *Athenian citizens showed their dislike for a politician by scratching his name on pieces of broken pottery known as* ostraka.

trade with their neighbours. Much of this trade involved luxury goods from Greece being exchanged for grain to help feed the Greek population.

One of the important trading colonies in the western Mediterranean was Massilia, on the site of present-day Marseilles. From here the Greeks could trade with the Celts who lived along the Rhone Valley, and objects from Greece have been found in the tombs of important people as far north as the Seine Valley.

◆ *Boys were taught how to read and write. They also learned music, poetry and mathematics. In contrast, girls stayed at home and learned how to look after the house and the family.*

figure to be removed from office, perhaps exiled too.

This was the first democracy, or government by the people. Although women and slaves had no vote, they could at least listen to political speeches in the *agora* or marketplace.

COLONIES

Cities such as Athens and Corinth may have had populations of between 50,000 and 100,000 people by the 5th century BC. As this led to overcrowding, colonies were set up in non-Greek lands around the Mediterranean, from which the Greeks could

◆ In Athens, speakers in the law courts were given a fixed amount of time to make their speeches. This device was used to time them. When all the water had run from the top container into the bottom one, the speaker's time was up.

Water clock

Doctor

◆ The Greeks were among the first people to separate medicine from religion. They realized that illness was caused by something in the body and was not a punishment from the gods. Dispensers sold medicines made from plants, just as pharmacists do today.

◆ Different views of society are depicted on Greek pottery. Many pots show heroic battles, events from the Olympic games or scenes from the *Iliad* or the *Odyssey*, but this one shows a slave helping her drunken master.

Decorated pottery

ALEXANDER THE GREAT

359–323 BC

After the Peloponnesian War, Sparta dominated Greece for a while. Sparta was crushed by Thebes in 371 BC, but Theban dominance lasted only until 359 BC, when 23-year-old Philip became king of Macedonia in northern Greece. He was determined to control the whole of Greece.

Philip made his army the strongest yet seen and used it in the continuing wars among the city-states. By allying himself with first one side and then another, he defeated them all.

In 336 BC, Philip was assassinated and his 20-year-old son, Alexander, came to the throne. Having crushed an attempt by the city-states to regain their independence and destroy Thebes, he found that all the wars had left the royal treasury empty. He decided to carry out his father's dream of conquering Persia and taking control of its rich empire.

He succeeded in this between 334 and 331 BC, and also added Egypt to his empire. In 325 BC he conquered eastern Iran and the Indus Valley, before his troops rebelled and forced him to go back to Babylon, which became the capital of his empire.

◆ *Alexander rode at the head of his troops and led charges on his famous horse, Bucephalus. A mosaic found among the ruins at Pompeii in Italy shows him leading his soldiers against the Persians at the battle of Issus.*

◆ *Greek influence can still be seen in these buildings in Petra which was part of Alexander's empire.*

the peoples of his empire and encouraged his soldiers to marry Persian women. He married Roxanne, the daughter of a nobleman from Bactria, and began to adopt Persian ways.

His armies did not like this and, after Alexander's death in 323 BC, ambitious generals killed his son, then fought for control of his empire. To prevent any of them gaining too much power, it was split into three states. Macedonian kings ruled in the north, the Seleucids ruled the Middle East, and the Ptolemies ruled Egypt.

◆ *Alexander marched east with his troops to reach as far as northwest India, where he defeated the Indian king, Poros, at the battle of Hydaspes.*

Alexander was more than a ruthless general. From the age of 13 he was taught for four years by Aristotle, the Athenian philosopher, and learned about botany and zoology. He valued knowledge and took scholars on his expeditions to study and write about different places. He tried, without success, to unite

◆ Alexander and his father used powerful catapults in their battles. These were strongly constructed from wood and had springs made **Catapult** from twisted gut or hair. The springs were wound up tightly and then released, to hurl the rocks from the containers.

Macedonian phalanx

◆ Philip armed his foot soldiers with pikes called *sarissas*, which were 5 metres long, and grouped them in a new type of phalanx. This contributed greatly to his success in expanding the Macedonian territory.

◆ Alexander was 32 years old when he died in Babylon and was buried in Alexandria, Egypt. He is said to have died of a fever, but some people think he may have been poisoned.

Gold coin showing Alexander

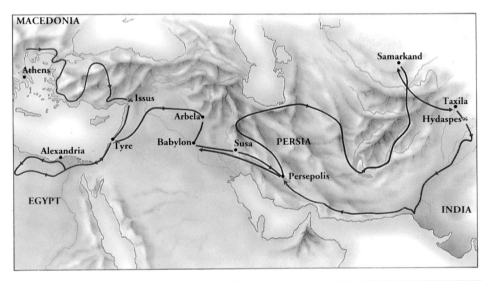

MACEDONIA

Athens

Issus

Arbela

Alexandria
Tyre
Babylon
Susa
PERSIA
Persepolis

EGYPT

Samarkand

Taxila
Hydaspes

INDIA

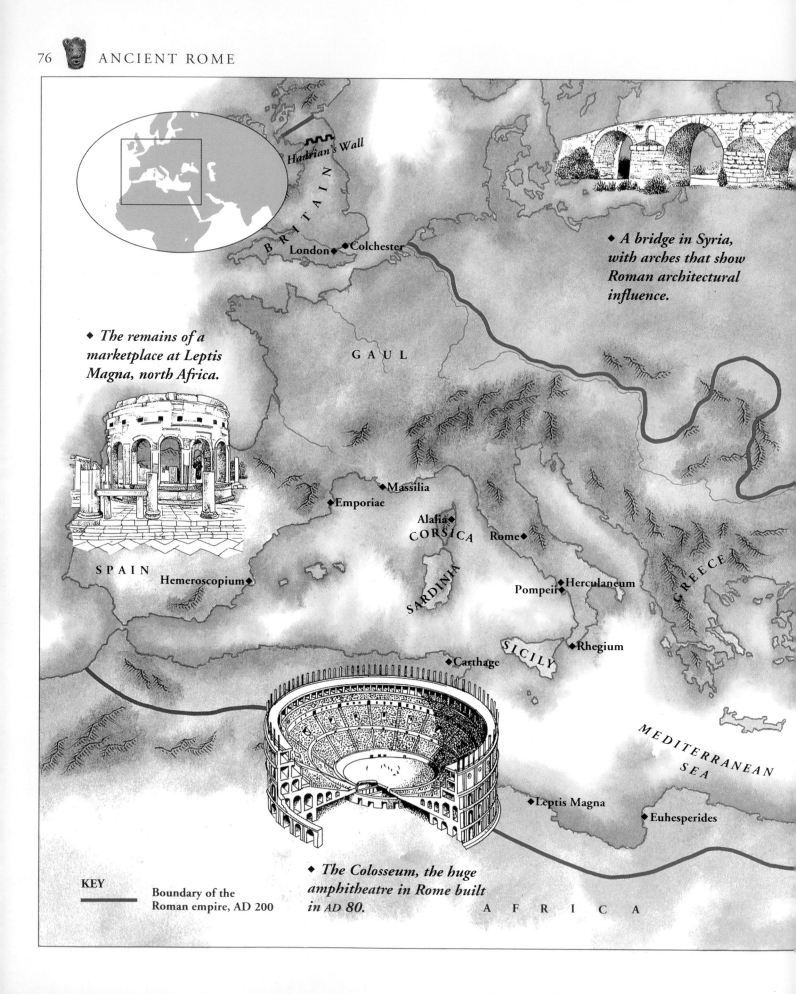

Hadrian's Wall

BRITAIN

London ◆ Colchester

GAUL

♦ A bridge in Syria, with arches that show Roman architectural influence.

♦ The remains of a marketplace at Leptis Magna, north Africa.

♦ Massilia

◆ Emporiae

Alalia ◆

CORSICA

Rome ◆

SPAIN

Hemeroscopium ◆

SARDINIA

Pompeii ◆ ♦ Herculaneum

GREECE

♦ Rhegium

SICILY

◆ Carthage

MEDITERRANEAN SEA

♦ Leptis Magna

♦ Euhesperides

KEY

———— Boundary of the Roman empire, AD 200

♦ The Colosseum, the huge amphitheatre in Rome built in AD 80.

AFRICA

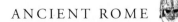

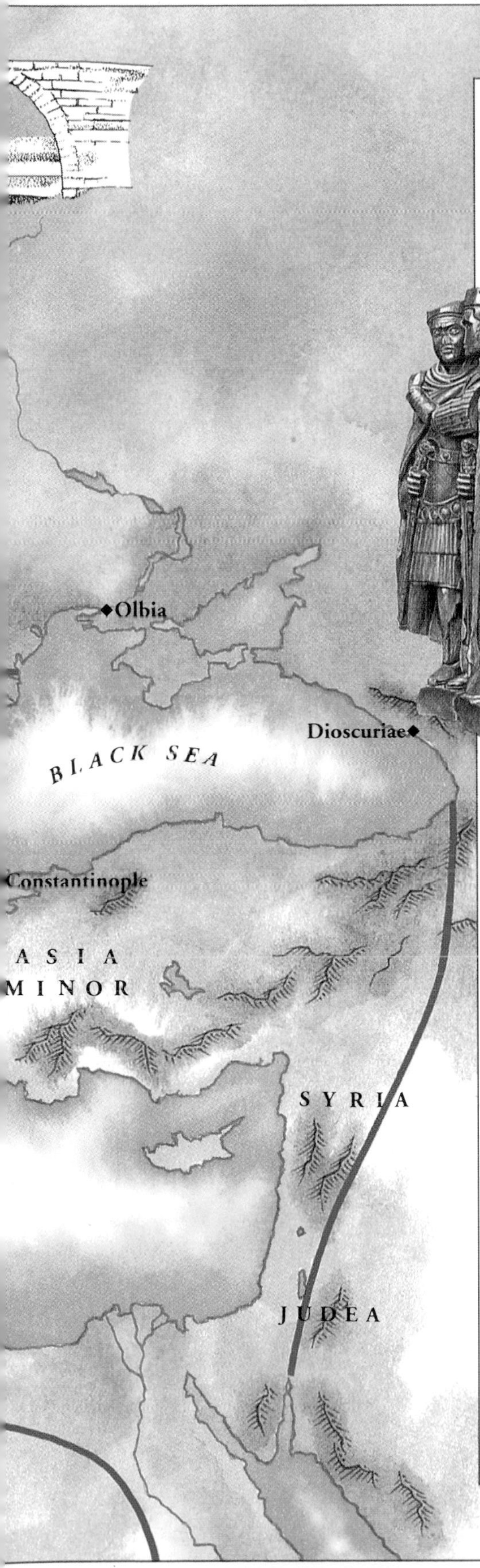

ANCIENT ROME

At the start of the 8th century BC many different tribes of people lived in what we now call Italy. Two of the most important tribes were the Etruscans and the Latins. Most of the people were farmers and lived in villages or on farms. The Etruscans were also traders, and they built towns and cities.

Rome itself started out as a collection of small villages on the banks of the Tiber River. The villages gradually united into one settlement and the people became known as Romans. As Rome became more powerful, it changed from being a kingdom to being a republic and then an empire.

At its greatest extent, this empire stretched from Asia Minor in the east to Britain and Portugal in the west and included all the lands around the Mediterranean. It contained about sixty million people, of whom 450,000 were in the army at any one time.

Olbia

Dioscuriae◆

BLACK SEA

Constantinople

ASIA MINOR

SYRIA

JUDEA

THE FOUNDATION OF ROME

753–510 BC

◆ The she-wolf from the story of Romulus and Remus became the symbol of the city of Rome.

Like many ancient peoples, the Romans wanted to trace the foundation of their city back to the gods. They did this through the story of the twin brothers Romulus and Remus, who were said to be descended from the Greek goddess Aphrodite and the Roman god Mars.

The twins were grandsons of King Numitor. Just after they were born, they were thrown into the Tiber River by a wicked great uncle, Amulius. He hoped they would drown, but they were washed ashore and saved by a she-wolf. A shepherd raised them as his sons until they were reunited with King Numitor.

When they grew up, they founded the city of Rome, but quarrelled over who would rule. Remus was killed by his brother in the fight and in 753 BC Romulus became king.

LATINS AND ETRUSCANS

In reality, early Rome probably developed from small farming villages on hills by the banks of the Tiber River. It grew into a city from around 750 BC onwards, when the marshland by the river was cleared to make a public square, and defensive walls were built around two of the hills.

◆ Wealthy Etruscans decorated their tombs with vivid paintings, which tell us a great deal about everyday life. Here, a flute player entertains guests at a banquet.

◆ *The Etruscans were skilled metal-workers, who used bronze, gold and iron to make useful and decorative objects, such as this tableware. The Romans often copied their designs.*

Rome was influenced by the older culture of the Etruscans, in north Italy, who in turn had been influenced by the Greeks and the city of Carthage. The inhabitants of early Rome were a mixture of Etruscans and *Latini*, or Latins, from south of Rome. Eventually they all became known as Romans. The Latin language dominated and the Etruscan tongue disappeared.

At first the city was ruled by a series of seven Etruscan kings. Each wore a cloak-like robe, called a *toga*, edged with purple. A symbol of his authority was the *fasces*: a bundle of rods with an axe attached.

The king's power was not absolute, nor was his title hereditary. Instead, an assembly of the people and a group of elders called the senate had a say in who became king and also in what he did.

One of the king's tasks was to raise an army to defend Rome. This was the beginning of the army which would eventually help Rome to win an empire and become a great power.

◆ *Iron-Age shepherds and farmers were the first settlers on the hills where Rome eventually grew up. They lived in huts built of straw, with wooden frames.*

◆ The bundle of wooden rods in the *fasces* represented the king's right to beat people if they had done wrong. The axe showed that he had power of life or death over them. When Rome became a republic, *fasces* continued to be the symbol of power.

Fasces

Etruscan alphabet

◆ Although the Etruscans' language died out and most examples of their writing disappeared, enough remain for us to know that they used an alphabet.

◆ Many Roman homes had an altar dedicated to a god. The head of the family prayed to it and made gifts of food, such as fruit and cheese.

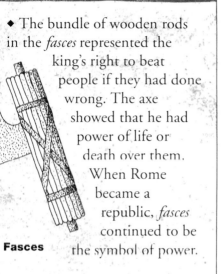

Household god

HEADING TOWARDS AN EMPIRE

510–27 BC

The kings of Rome may have thought they were Etruscans, rather than Romans, but by 510 BC Rome had grown large enough to want its own rulers. The king was driven out and Rome became a republic, ruled by the senate.

First, the senate had to deal with the problem that Rome was being threatened by its neighbours. Also, in the city itself, there was trouble between patricians and plebians. Patricians were wealthy landowners who had a say in government, and plebians were the peasants, workers and traders who made up the mass of the population but were not allowed to hold public office.

Roman power began to grow, greatly helped by a large and professional army, a good climate for successful farming, and easy access to deposits of copper, silver, iron and lead ores for making tools and weapons. The Romans relied on a plentiful supply of slaves to work in the mines and do other dirty or dangerous work.

PUNIC WARS

In 264 BC, war broke out between Rome and Carthage over power in the Mediterranean. When this First Punic War ended in 241 BC, Rome had won control of the seas around Sicily, Corsica and Sardinia. Wanting revenge, the Carthaginian general Hannibal started the Second Punic War in 218 BC, by marching on Rome. He was eventually defeated in 201 BC. In the Third Punic War, from 149 to 146 BC, the Romans finally destroyed the power of Carthage and took control of north Africa.

CONQUERING THE CELTS

Long before the start of the Punic Wars, the Romans had traded with the Celts, whom they called Gauls. Through this trade, they

◆ *With the help of the Celts, Hannibal took his army and his war elephants over the Alps to attack Rome from the north in 218 BC.*

◆ *The senate in Rome was made up of elders from the patrician class who were known as senators. Each year they elected two consuls (top left) to lead them. The consuls had a lot of authority. When Julius Caesar declared himself dictator he became 'first among equals' (below left).*

JULIUS CAESAR

Julius Caesar was an aristocrat who was elected consul in 60 BC. He was a skilful and ambitious general who soon conquered more territory for Rome, including the rest of France. In 49 BC he returned to Rome and five years later he declared himself dictator for life, even though Rome was still a republic. He was assassinated in that same year, but in 27 BC his nephew and heir, Octavian, became the first emperor and took the new name of Augustus.

knew that the Celtic lands were rich. The Celts, however, managed to defeat the Roman army and attacked Rome itself in around 390 BC. There were more clashes after this date, but in 225 BC the Roman army defeated the Celts at the battle of Telamon.

In 224 BC the Romans invaded what is now southeast France, but their plans were halted briefly by the outbreak of the Second Punic War. From 198 BC, however, the conquest began again. They took control of Spain and by 121 BC they had conquered the whole of southern France.

◆ *The eagle on top of this standard was the symbol of Rome and its power. Each legion of the army had its own standard which was carried into battle. It was thought to be a disgrace if the standard was captured by the enemy.*

◆ From earliest times, the Romans traded with their neighbours. They exported wine in huge pottery jars, or *amphorae*, in exchange for other goods.

Amphora

Testudo formation

◆ Roman soldiers sometimes fought in a formation known as the *testudo* ('tortoise'), in which their shields were carried over their heads like a tortoise's shell. This made it difficult for the enemy to kill or injure them.

◆ A Roman soldier wore armour on top of a thick woollen tunic. He also had a sword, a dagger and a shield.

Roman foot soldier

LIFE IN THE ROMAN EMPIRE

27 BC–AD 250

The Romans took their civilization to all the countries that they added to their empire. But they tried not to upset the local way of life too much, as they wanted to live in peace with the people they had conquered. So long as these people were prepared to respect Roman gods and Roman laws, they were allowed to keep many of their own traditions.

The situation was made easier by the fact that many of the conquered peoples already knew about the Roman way of life through trading contacts. Some of them were only too pleased to become Romanized and accept what the empire had to offer.

The Romans built a system of good paved roads between the major cities. They were built mainly for military use, to allow the army to travel quickly in times of trouble, but were also used by people travelling for trade or for pleasure.

◆ *At its greatest extent, the empire provided the Romans with everything they needed, including slaves. This one was portrayed in a mosaic found at Pompeii.*

NEW TOWNS

Military camps and permanent forts for the army were built along the new roads, and towns often developed near or around these. Other towns grew up where two roads crossed or joined each other.

◆ *All Roman towns and cities had public baths where people went to bathe or simply to sit and gossip. Men and women had separate baths in large towns or went at different times in smaller towns.*

◆ *Roman roads were built of layers of gravel, rubble, concrete and paving. The surfaces were curved, so that rainwater ran off them into roadside ditches.*

The towns were well planned, with many public buildings and open spaces, as well as houses, apartment blocks, workshops, food stores, taverns and restaurants where families could eat out. Not all Roman houses had many cooking facilities.

The public buildings included a theatre and an amphitheatre, and at least one bath house, which usually had a *palaestra,* or open courtyard, where people could exercise. There were also government buildings and a *basilica,* or large hall, where meetings were held.

Judges sat inside the basilica to consider different legal cases,

relating to the state and to individuals. Next door to it was a building called the *curia.* This was where the councillors met to pass local laws and to arrange how taxes would be collected. Above them were two magistrates, called *duoviri,* who held office for a year and governed the town.

All business in the town stopped around noon, and in the hottest weather people took a rest. The poor went back to work later, while the rich had the rest of the day off.

◆ *Chariot racing was a popular spectator sport. The chariots were very light, and one of the charioteer's main tasks was to keep balance, especially when taking a corner. Inevitably, there were many accidents and crashes.*

◆ Buildings were heated by a hypocaust. The floors were raised on pillars to create a space underneath. Heat from an adjoining furnace was circulated through the space to warm the room above.

Hypocaust, showing flow of warm air

◆ Pompeii, in southwest Italy, was overwhelmed by volcanic ash from Mount Vesuvius in AD 79. The ash hardened around everything it fell on, and preserved the town as it looked when it was destroyed.

◆ Octavian was the first Roman emperor. His 41-year reign was a time of peace and prosperity at home, and steady expansion abroad. He was renamed Augustus, which means 'imposing one', and, after his death in AD 14, proclaimed to be a god.

Augustus

Fountain at Pompeii

◆ Only the wealthy had water piped to their homes in Roman towns, but there were many public fountains. This waterspout is carved with the face of a water god.

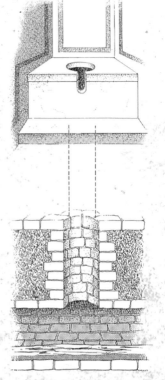

Public lavatory

◆ Many Roman towns had communal public lavatories. The seats were set over brick-lined drains where water ran to take the waste away.

◆ *Important public buildings in a Roman town included (1) the forum; (2) the temple; (3) the circus; (4) the baths and (5) the theatre. Towns were defended by stout walls with four main gates (6).*

THE FORUM

Most of the government buildings in a town, and also many of the temples, were grouped around the *forum*, an open area with covered pavements where people could meet and talk in all kinds of weather. Each temple was dedicated to a different god or goddess. Many of the Roman deities were the same as the Greek ones, but with different names. For example, the Roman goddess Diana was the same as the Greek goddess Artemis. Jupiter was the same as Zeus and Neptune the same as Poseidon. People thought of a temple as a house for the particular god or goddess, whose statue was kept there. Priests and priestesses carried out ceremonies and made animal sacrifices to the deity. Ordinary people made promises to different gods in exchange for their help.

◆ *Shops and taverns lined the main Roman streets. Shoppers and schoolchildren mixed with people carrying water home from the public water trough.*

Schools were usually set up in private houses and parents had to pay a fee for their children to attend. Many more boys than girls went to school, but evidence from letters and wax tablets shows that some women could read and write.

A Life of Luxury

Life in the Roman empire was luxurious for the rich. Their town houses were large, private and well furnished and they had many slaves to help with the work. Many wealthy people also had a country villa or an estate where they could go for relaxation.

Wealthy women wore make-up and perfume and dressed in clothes made from silk and fine linen. They probably helped choose the decorations for their houses. These included frescoes and mosaics.

Not everyone was pleased to be part of the Roman empire. Many people wanted to keep their independence and live by their own laws. Rebellions broke out at various times in Spain, Gaul, Britain and Judea. The Romans always crushed the rebels, often with great loss of life on both sides. For example, during the main British rebellion against the Romans in AD 61, up to 60,000 people died and the Roman towns of Colchester and London were badly damaged.

◆ If there was not enough water for everyone living in a Roman town, civil engineers brought in more from the surrounding area through channels and pipes. Because water cannot flow uphill, the engineers built huge bridges, called aqueducts, to carry the water pipes across valleys.

The Romans also thought that their emperors became gods when they died and so temples were dedicated to them, too.

Children in towns were able to go to school from the age of seven. They learned to read and write and do arithmetic, before moving on to study history, geometry and literature at the age of 11.

THE DECLINE OF THE ROMAN EMPIRE

AD 250–500

The decline of the Roman empire began in the 3rd century AD. Central government weakened as a series of emperors was assassinated or removed from power by the army. Frontiers came under attack, so crippling taxes were demanded to pay for stronger defences and more soldiers.

In AD 286 the emperor Diocletian decided that the empire was too big for one man to rule by himself. He appointed a co-emperor to rule the western half while he ruled the east. He reorganized and expanded the army and imposed a system of taxation to help to pay for it.

Diocletian also subdivided the provinces to make them easier to rule. On a personal level, he persecuted people who did not believe that the emperor had divine authority and became a god when he died. He viewed such people as a threat to the security of the empire.

◆ *Feeling threatened by outsiders, the Romans began to build stronger defences around their towns and cities. Every town was protected by a massive defensive wall, and could only be entered through a gatehouse.*

◆ Diocletian suggested a tetrarchy, or 'rule of four', to administer the vast empire. The co-emperors were each helped by a lieutenant.

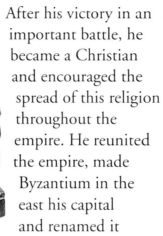

CONSTANTINE

Constantine the Great was emperor from AD 306 to AD 337. During his reign he reversed many of Diocletian's policies.

After his victory in an important battle, he became a Christian and encouraged the spread of this religion throughout the empire. He reunited the empire, made Byzantium in the east his capital and renamed it Constantinople. Soon it became as grand as Rome itself.

The western half of the empire became weaker in the 5th century, and parts were overrun by people the Romans called Barbarians. They set up their own kingdoms within the empire and in AD 410 they attacked the city of Rome.

Soon after this the western half of the Roman empire finally collapsed, but that in the east continued and became known as the Byzantine empire.

◆ Hadrian's Wall across the north of England marked the northwest boundary of the Roman empire. It was built in AD 122-126 as a defence against the Picts from the north.

◆ The alphabets used in many parts of the world today developed from the Roman alphabet. This makes it fairly easy for us to decipher Roman inscriptions. This slave tag says: "Hold me, in case I flee, and return me to my master Viventius of the estate of Callistus."

Bronze slave tag

Roman house

◆ Roman houses were usually built of brick or stone and had tiled roofs. In big cities some people lived in cramped apartment blocks up to three storeys high.

◆ The emperor Constantine came to power in AD 306. He was proclaimed emperor by his troops. By 330 he had moved the capital of the empire to Byzantium, calling it Constantinople.

Imperial portrait

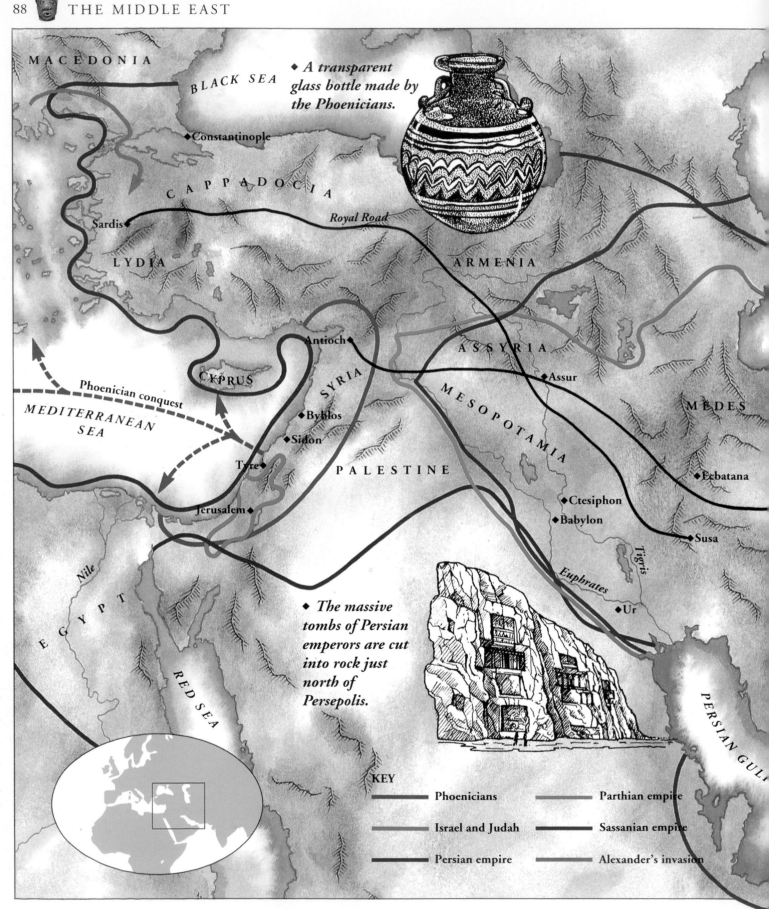

MACEDONIA

BLACK SEA

◆ *A transparent glass bottle made by the Phoenicians.*

◆ Constantinople

C A P P A D O C I A

Royal Road

Sardis ◆

LYDIA

ARMENIA

Antioch ◆

ASSYRIA

CYPRUS

SYRIA

Assur ◆

Phoenician conquest

M E S O P O T A M I A

MEDES

MEDITERRANEAN SEA

◆ Byblos

◆ Sidon

PALESTINE

Ecbatana ◆

Tyre ◆

Ctesiphon ◆

Babylon ◆

Jerusalem ◆

Susa ◆

Tigris

Nile

Euphrates

EGYPT

◆ *The massive tombs of Persian emperors are cut into rock just north of Persepolis.*

Ur ◆

RED SEA

PERSIAN GULF

KEY

———	Phoenicians	———	Parthian empire
———	Israel and Judah	———	Sassanian empire
———	Persian empire	———	Alexander's invasion

ARAL SEA

CASPIAN SEA

PARTHIANS

Silk Road

PERSIA

SASSANIANS

◆Persepolis

THE MIDDLE EAST

The Middle East had hot summers and cold winters. Some parts received little or no rain. Although grain crops, olives and grapes could be grown in many places, not everyone made their living from farming.

In the semi-arid places, nomadic herders and their families looked after camels and sheep. Towns attracted craftworkers, merchants and traders. These traders had contacts with all parts of the then-known world, and went on long journeys by sea and land to obtain luxury goods such as silk from China.

The geography of the Middle East led to the development of small countries and city-states in the area between the Syrian desert and the Mediterranean. In the east, however, large empires appeared. The earliest was the Persian, or Achaemenid, empire. Alexander the Great conquered this empire, together with the rest of the Middle East, and after his death in 323 BC it was taken over by the Seleucids.

THE PHOENICIAN CIVILIZATION

2750–146 BC

◆ *A priestess from the Phoenician city of Carthage. According to legend, the city of Carthage was founded by Dido, daughter of a king of Tyre.*

In the third millennium BC, the Phoenician civilization developed at the eastern end of the Mediterranean, in an area that is now part of Syria, Lebanon and Israel. The Phoenicians lived in the land of Canaan until 1200 BC, and spoke a language related to both Babylonian and Hebrew. They were originally known as Canaanites, but from around 1200 BC they became Phoenicians, from the Greek word *phoinos*, meaning 'red', which was the colour of a dye they exported.

Although the Phoenicians grew grapes, olives and grain crops, and kept sheep and cattle, there was not enough fertile land for everyone to farm. Many Phoenicians earned their living by trade and seafaring, building sturdy boats from cedar and pine trees.

Each Phoenician city was an independent state, sometimes in alliance with another, but usually acting by itself. The three main cities were Tyre, Sidon and Byblos. They attracted skilled craftworkers, shipbuilders and merchants.

IVORY AND GLASS

The Phoenicians were skilled at working with ivory, and invented the process of glass-blowing. They were the first people to make transparent glass on a large scale. They also produced an expensive reddish-purple dye, and cloth dyed with this was highly valued in Greece and Rome.

The objects they made were traded with other countries. Goods from all parts of the then-known world

◆ *Ivory carving was a craft at which the Phoenicians excelled. They got the ivory in Egypt, from elephant tusks which had been transported north along the Nile.*

changed hands in Phoenician ports: fine weapons and jewellery, as well as wine from Rome and silks from China.

TRADING COLONIES

As the Phoenicians gained wealth and power, they set up trading colonies on the islands of Cyprus, Crete, Malta, Sicily, Sardinia, Corsica and the Balearics. They also set up colonies on the mainland shores of the Mediterranean, including Tangiers and Carthage (in north Africa) and Cadiz (in southern Spain). From these they could trade with places as far away as Britain and the west coast of Africa, as well as with Egypt, Rome and Greece.

CARTHAGE

The legend of Carthage claims that when Dido landed in north Africa, she asked the local ruler for some land. He said she could have as much as she could cover with an ox-hide, so she cut it into thin strips and marked out a large area. Carthage was built on this site and in the 3rd century bc, it was vying with Rome for control of the Mediterranean. This lead to the Punic Wars, whose name comes from the Roman word for Phoenicians.

In 146 BC, after over 100 years of enmity, Rome destroyed Carthage, and the Phoenician civilization started to decline.

◆ The Carthaginians traded with Africans on an island off the coast of Senegal. The island was chosen because it was neutral territory. The two peoples did not speak the same language, so they bargained with each other using sign language instead of speech.

◆ The reddish-purple dye for which the Phoenicians were famous was produced from a gland in a sea snail called the murex. Extracting the glands was a smelly process, and was said to make the city of Tyre reek of garlic.

Murex

◆ The Phoenicians were among the first people to use an alphabet, rather than pictograms or hieroglyphs. It was made up of 30 letters, all of which were consonants.

Phoenician alphabet

◆ The Phoenicians developed close links with the Israelites. When Solomon built the first Temple in Jerusalem, the king of Tyre supplied him with craftworkers and with timber from cedars of Lebanon.

Cedar of Lebanon

THE HEBREWS AND THE LAND OF ISRAEL

2000–683 BC

The Hebrews moved from southern Mesopotamia to settle in Palestine around 2000 BC. Their name comes from the ancient Greek version of the Hebrew word for 'people from the other side' (of the Euphrates). Much of the history of these people is known from the Bible. Their story begins in Genesis, the first book of the Old Testament, with Abraham.

ABRAHAM AND JACOB

The Bible tells us that Abraham was a shepherd from Ur, who brought his family to settle in Canaan. Abraham's grandson Jacob had 12 sons, from whom 12 Hebrew tribes are said to have come. Jacob was also known as Israel, and, eventually, the Hebrews were called Israelites after him.

When Canaan was hit by a severe famine, Jacob and his family went to Egypt.

Some time after their arrival, they were enslaved and suffered dreadful hardships. At one time all the male children were murdered, at the command of the Egyptian pharaoh.

One child to escape this slaughter was Moses. He grew up to be a religious leader and took his people out of Egypt, back towards Canaan, which he called the Promised Land. The journey took 40 years. The Bible describes how, during this time, Moses received his god Yahweh's commandments on Mount Sinai. It also tells that he died, east of the Jordan River, before the Israelites reached Canaan.

◆ *Making bricks was one of the tasks that the Hebrew slaves had to carry out in Egypt. The bricks were made from mud, clay and chopped straw, all mixed together by hand.*

◆ *The Temple in Jerusalem was a place of pilgrimage and worship. Richly decorated and furnished, it stood in a fortified enclosure. Priests directed the worship which was accompanied by music. Animal sacrifices were also made there.*

Those who did reach Canaan had to fight against the Philistines before they were able to settle there again. They established a land which came to be called Israel.

THE KINGS OF ISRAEL

The fight against the Philistines continued, but from around 1020 BC Israel began to prosper, first under King Saul and then under King David. During David's reign, Israel became a major power in western Asia. The Philistines were finally defeated and the 12 tribes united into one nation, with the capital established at Jerusalem.

The next king was Solomon. He developed a system of law and set up trade links with other countries. He also built the first Temple in Jerusalem for the followers of Yahweh.

Solomon introduced high taxes and compulsory labour. Many of his people rebelled against this and, after his death, his kingdom split into two, with Israel in the north and Judah, with Jerusalem as its capital, in the south. The Assyrians captured Israel in 722 BC and Judah in 683 BC, and the people then became known as Jews.

These first five books of the Bible are called the *Torah,* and tradition holds that they were written by Moses. Others claim that they were passed down by word of mouth and first written down in the time of Solomon, or later. The *Torah* is the basis of Judaism.

◆ Solomon was famed for his wisdom. To help him manage the large kingdom his father had left him, he divided Israel into 12 districts, each with its own governor. He also built up good relationships with neighbouring states, bringing peace and prosperity to Israel.

Solomon

Ark of the Covenant

◆ The Ten Commandments, as given to Moses, were kept in the Ark of the Covenant in the Temple in Jerusalem.

◆ The Philistines settled in Canaan after being forced out of Egypt. They strongly resisted the Israelites when they in turn returned from Egypt. The part of Canaan where they lived was named Palestine after them.

Philistine burial jar

THE MIGHTY PERSIAN EMPIRE

551–330 BC

Persia is the old name for the land we call Iran. The name comes from the Persians who, together with the Medes, migrated there from the east in around 1300 BC.

At first the Medes were the more powerful, but in 551 BC, Cyrus, ruler of the Persian province of Anshan, rebelled and defeated them. He made Ecbatana his capital and began to build an empire. He had an army of cavalrymen and archers, and by 530 BC, when he was killed in battle, his lands stretched from the Mediterranean to Afghanistan and from the Arabian Sea to the Caspian and Aral Seas. There was an unsuccessful attempt to conquer Greece, under the command of Darius I who came to power in 521 BC, but the Persian empire did include Egypt and the Indus Valley.

◆ *An image of Darius I, hunting a lion from his chariot. The god Ahura Mazda watches over him.*

DARIUS THE GREAT

Darius's official title was *shahanshah*, which means 'king of kings'. He was a good general, who tried to increase the prosperity of his land. Darius made Persepolis the royal centre of

◆ *People from all parts of the empire came to Persepolis with gifts and tribute for the king.*

◆ *From carvings which can still be seen on the palace steps, archaeologists know that the tribute paid at Persepolis included food, animals, fine cloth, gold and jewels.*

his empire, and Susa the administrative centre. He divided the empire into 20 satrapies, or provinces, with good roads between them. To pay for these, he levied taxes and demanded tribute from his many subjects.

Agriculture was important and new irrigation schemes were set up to make it possible to grow more crops, adding to the empire's wealth.

The Persian empire is sometimes referred to as the Achaemenid empire, after one of its dynasties. It lasted until 330 BC when Alexander the Great defeated Darius III and took control of his lands.

◆ *Many soldiers defended the king and the vast stores of tribute kept at the palace.*

◆ Mithras was the Persian god of light, truth and justice. According to legend, he killed a magic bull, and every animal and plant sprang out of its blood. He was also worshipped by Roman soldiers.

Mithras

◆ Zoroastrianism was founded by the Persian prophet Zarathustra in the 6th century BC. He taught that the one supreme god, Ahura Mazda, battles against evil. The religion still survives today in remote parts of India and Iran.

◆ This silver drinking cup from the 5th century BC shows a griffin, a fabulous creature in Persian mythology.

Silver drinking cup

THE PARTHIAN AND SASSANIAN EMPIRE

250 BC–AD 350

The Parthians were nomadic people from east of the Caspian Sea. They moved into Persia and lived first under Persian rule, then under Alexander the Great. From 323 BC they were under Seleucid rule, until, in around 250 BC, the Parthian governor set up an independent kingdom.

The new capital was at Ctesiphon. Society was probably feudal, with everything belonging to the king. The army included mounted archers and heavily armoured men called cataphracts. Horses, too, were protected with chainmail. The cavalry trained by playing an early form of polo, with up to 100 people on each side. The last Parthian king was killed in AD 224 by Ardashir who founded the Sassanian dynasty.

◆ The Parthian cavalry often tricked their enemies into defeat by first riding away, as if in retreat from the battle. When the enemy pursued them, however, they skilfully turned around in the saddle and fired their arrows backwards.

THE SASSANIANS

At its greatest, the Sassanian empire stretched from Syria to India. Its art and architecture followed Persian designs. Zoroastrianism became the state religion. Like the Parthians, the Sassanians depended heavily on agriculture, camels and sheep, and more wealth came from trade. Works of art were exported to China, where over 1,200 Sassanian coins have been found.

Parthians and Sassanians opposed the Roman empire. In AD 260 the Sassanian ruler Shapur I captured the Roman emperor Valerian. He went on to conquer Armenia and invade the Roman provinces of Syria and Cappadocia. After his death in AD 273, there was greater peace between the two empires.

◆ Both dromedaries and Bactrian camels were domesticated by 2000 BC. Because they could graze on poor land at the edge of deserts and carry heavy loads, they were used for transporting goods along the Silk Road.

◆ Shapur I forced the Roman emperor Valerian to submit to him. After this, he is said to have had Valerian's body skinned, stuffed and put on display.

Fire temple

◆ Remains of Zoroastrian fire temples have been found throughout the Sassanian empire. They were built to house the Atar Gushnasp, the sacred fire of the warriors.

Shapur's palace

◆ Shapur I was probably the greatest Sassanian ruler. He made his capital at Ctesiphon, on the east bank of the Tigris River, and had a huge palace built for himself there.

◆ Skillful Sassanian craftworkers made beautiful objects from precious metals, gemstones and glass. Many of them were decorated with figures of people, animals and plants shown in relief, which made them stand out from the background.

THE LANDS OF PALESTINE AND JUDEA

597 BC–AD 73

In 597 BC the Babylonian king, Nebuchadnezzar, conquered Jerusalem. He destroyed the Temple built by Solomon, and exiled many Jews from Palestine to Babylon, where they lived in slavery. In exile the Jews continued to worship the one god Yahweh, build synagogues to pray in, and observe the strict laws set out by their religion.

When Babylon became part of the Persian empire, the Persian king, Cyrus, allowed a group of Jews to return to Jerusalem. They arrived there in 538 BC and rebuilt the Temple. Although Palestine was part of the Persian empire, the Jews were allowed to govern themselves to a large extent, according to their Jewish law and beliefs.

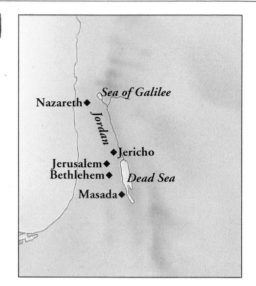

◆ *Major areas and towns in Palestine during the Roman occupation.*

SELEUCID RULE

Palestine was briefly part of Alexander the Great's empire. After his death, it came under the control of the Seleucids. Jews feared that the Seleucids would destroy their traditions.

In 167 BC Judas Maccabeus led a revolt against Antiochus IV, the Seleucid king who was trying to make Judaism illegal and force Greek religion on the Jews. The revolt continued until 141 BC, when the Jews liberated Jerusalem and Judea (formerly known as Judah) became independent.

◆ *Masada is a steep, rocky hilltop near the west coast of the Red Sea. During the revolt against Roman rule, the Jews were besieged there for almost two years.*

ROMAN RULE

In 63 BC, Judea was conquered by Rome and became part of the Roman empire. The Romans made Herod king of Judea in 37 BC, but although he was a Jew he was not popular. Many Jews left to settle in other parts of the Roman empire (some as far away as western India), but they still looked on Judea as their homeland.

♦ *The Temple in Jerusalem was rebuilt in the late 6th century BC. It was later restored by the Jewish leaders (the Maccabees) and then enlarged and expanded by King Herod. A great platform was built for the Temple, and it was surrounded by massive walls. Herod hoped this action would help to make the Jews more content with Roman rule.*

In AD 26, the Romans made Pontius Pilate governor of Judea. He often clashed with the Jews, and in AD 34 the Romans dismissed him. The difficult times continued for the Jews, however, and in AD 66 they started a great rebellion against Roman rule. At first they managed to drive the Romans out of Jerusalem, but Roman forces, led by Titus, recaptured the city in AD 70.

Jerusalem was then destroyed, and the Temple almost destroyed by fire. The rebellion lasted for another four years, ending only in AD 73, when the last of the Jewish forces committed mass suicide at the rocky stronghold of Masada, rather than surrender. After this, the Jews moved into exile, gradually spreading all over Europe and northern Africa.

Romans sacking the Temple

♦ The Romans destroyed the Temple in AD 70 during the Jewish revolt against their rule. In the 4th century AD an attempt was made to rebuild it, but it was abandoned.

♦ The many-branched candlestick, symbolizing, among other things, the seven days of creation, is called a *menorah*. The Romans carried one from the Temple in Jerusalem as it was destroyed. Menorahs are still used in the Jewish festival of Hanukkah today.

♦ The Star of David, or Shield of David, is a symbol of the Jewish faith. The figure itself is around 3,000 years old, although the term Shield of David dates from the 3rd century AD. The star appears on the flag of Israel.

Star of David

THE SPREAD OF CHRISTIANITY

5 BC–AD 350

Jesus was born in Bethlehem, in the Roman province of Judea, in about 5 BC, and grew up in Nazareth. For many years the Jews had believed that a Messiah, or Saviour, would come to lead them to freedom. When Jesus started to preach, his followers became sure that he was the Messiah and Son of God.

Jesus spoke about the coming of the kingdom of God, and told his followers how to make themselves worthy of entering it. He criticized the religious authorities in Judea, and talked of himself as the Messiah.

His followers accepted this, but other Jews accused him of blasphemy. They demanded that he be tried for this crime, in front of the Roman governor, Pontius Pilate.

At the same time, there was much unrest in Judea, because people were unhappy with Roman rule. The Romans were worried and saw the large crowds that gathered around Jesus as a threat to their authority. They therefore had Jesus arrested and put to death by crucifixion.

Three days later, news spread that Jesus had risen from the dead, and that all who believed in him would do the same. Belief in the resurrection formed the basis for a new religion, called Christianity from the Greek word *Christos*, 'anointed one'.

♦ *Jesus grew up in the town of Nazareth, where he probably worked as a carpenter. He began preaching and healing when he was about 32 years old. The story of his life and teachings appears in the New Testament of the Bible.*

♦ *Early Christians prayed in secret, for fear of persecution. In Rome they met in the catacombs under the city, where the dead were buried in niches in the walls of narrow passageways.*

The Dead Sea Scrolls
At the time that Jesus was teaching in Palestine, there were several Jewish sects. In 1947, ancient scrolls, thought to be from the library of one of the sects, were discovered in caves near the Dead Sea. Some 500 scrolls have been found, dating from about 250 BC to AD 70. They contain texts for almost all the books of the Old Testament, prayers and psalms. They tell us much about life in a Jewish community in the time of Jesus.

The followers of Jesus spread his teachings wherever they went. Among them were Peter, who founded churches in Palestine, and Paul, who went on three missionary journeys beyond Judea, taking Christianity to the Gentiles, or non-Jews.

IN ANCIENT ROME

By the 3rd century AD, the new religion had reached most parts of the Roman empire. The authorities viewed the Christians as rebels, who would not believe that the emperor became a god when he died. But it was not until AD 250 that they were persecuted on a large scale. Many were put to death in the arena, as part of public entertainments.

Many Christians therefore worshipped in secret until AD 313, when the emperor Constantine made Christianity legal, following his own conversion. In AD 325 he organized the first general church council, to establish a uniform doctrine throughout the Roman empire.

Christianity began to spread openly in AD 392, when it became the official religion of the empire.

♦ While their religion was illegal, Christians often made a sign like a fish to identify themselves to one another. They would draw it with a finger in sand or soil and then quickly cover it over.

♦ Monasticism is a form of religious life in which people choose to live apart from the everyday world so that they can devote themselves to prayer. Christian monasticism began in Egypt in AD 271, when Saint Anthony of Thebes went into the desert to lead a holier life. Other hermits gathered in desert monasteries during the 300s.

Cross

♦ The chi-rho sign was a symbol of Christianity. It was made up of the Greek letters for Ch and R, which are the first letters of Christ. The sign has been found on many objects throughout the Roman empire, such as this laurel wreath.

Chi-rho sign

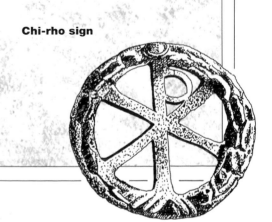

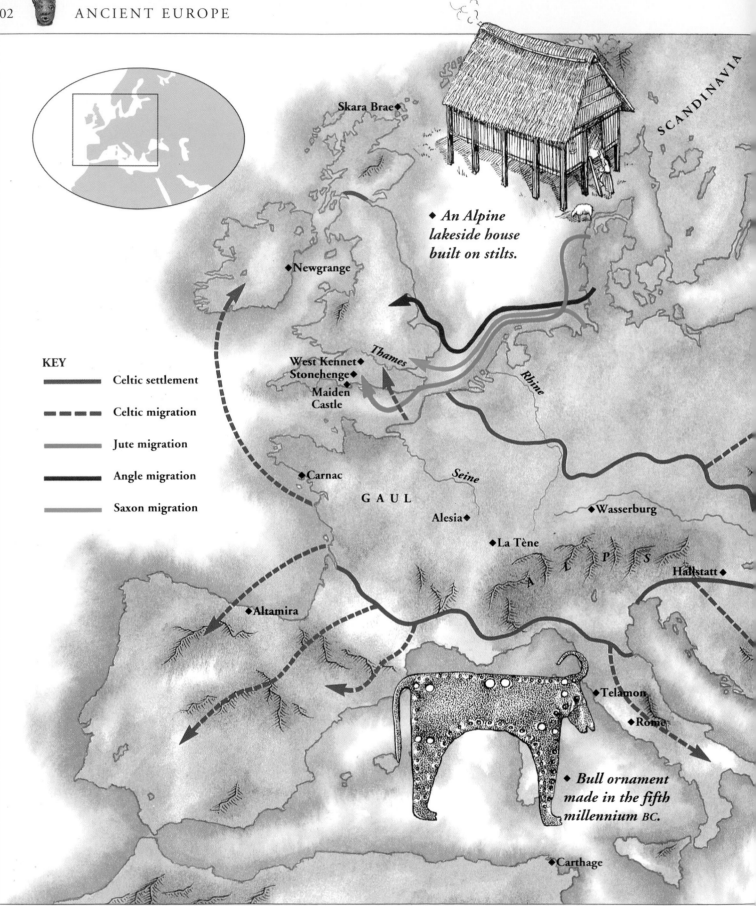

KEY

	Celtic settlement
	Celtic migration
	Jute migration
	Angle migration
	Saxon migration

Skara Brae◆

Newgrange◆

◆ *An Alpine lakeside house built on stilts.*

Thames

West Kennet◆
Stonehenge◆
Maiden
Castle◆

Rhine

◆Carnac

Seine

G A U L

Alesia◆

◆Wasserburg

◆La Tène

A L P S

Hallstatt ◆

SCANDINAVIA

◆Altamira

◆Telamon

◆Rome

◆ *Bull ornament made in the fifth millennium BC.*

◆Carthage

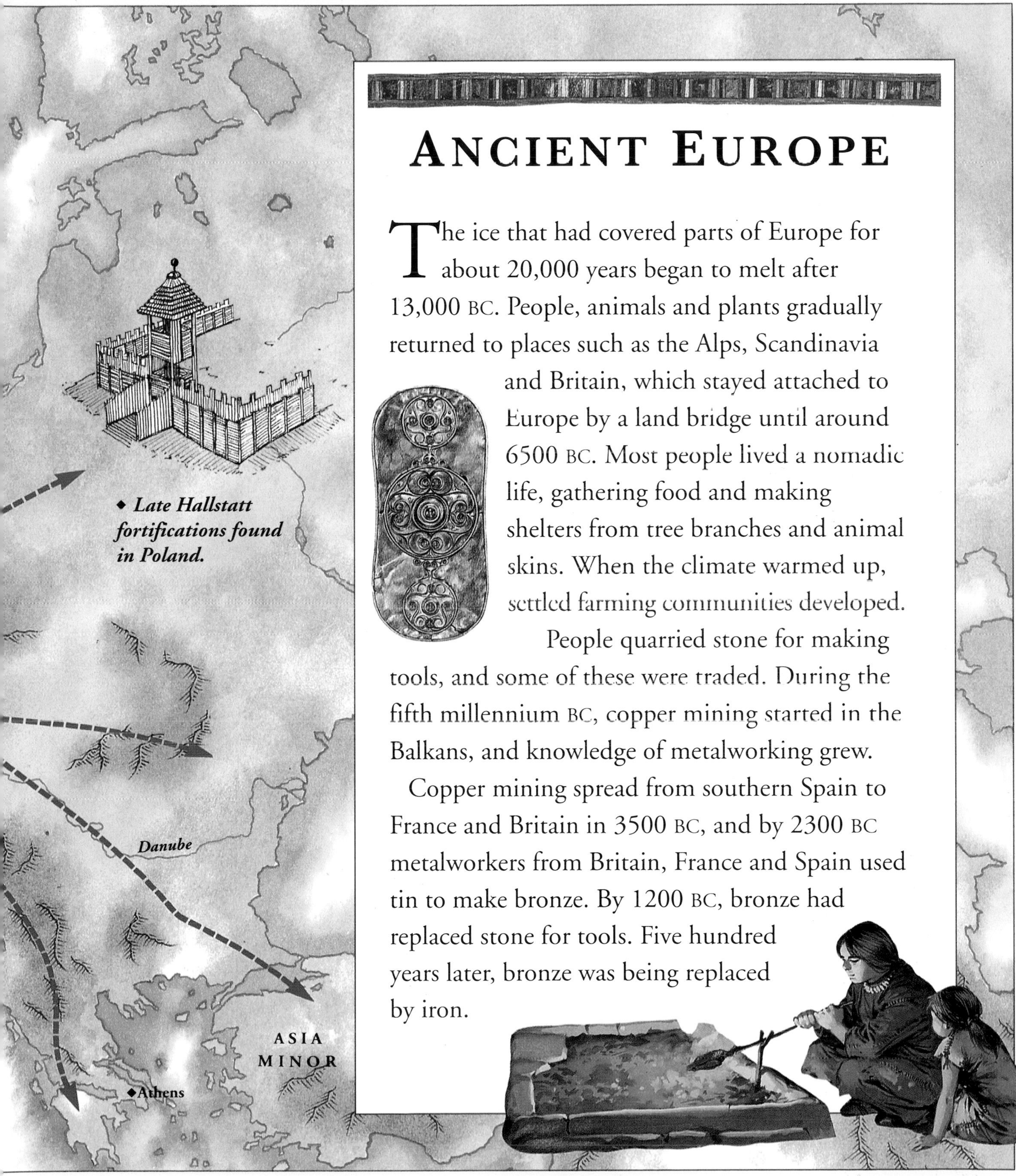

ANCIENT EUROPE

The ice that had covered parts of Europe for about 20,000 years began to melt after 13,000 BC. People, animals and plants gradually returned to places such as the Alps, Scandinavia and Britain, which stayed attached to Europe by a land bridge until around 6500 BC. Most people lived a nomadic life, gathering food and making shelters from tree branches and animal skins. When the climate warmed up, settled farming communities developed.

People quarried stone for making tools, and some of these were traded. During the fifth millennium BC, copper mining started in the Balkans, and knowledge of metalworking grew.

Copper mining spread from southern Spain to France and Britain in 3500 BC, and by 2300 BC metalworkers from Britain, France and Spain used tin to make bronze. By 1200 BC, bronze had replaced stone for tools. Five hundred years later, bronze was being replaced by iron.

◆ *Late Hallstatt fortifications found in Poland.*

Danube

ASIA MINOR

◆Athens

THE MONUMENTS OF MEGALITHIC EUROPE

4500–1500 BC

Farming spread through northern Europe from the southeast, but the small communities were not always permanent, so they left little evidence of their existence: some broken pottery, a few stone tools and weapons, and animal bones. Wooden houses have left little trace, except in some places in the Alps, where rising water levels have preserved the timbers of houses built on the lakesides.

Much more remains at Skara Brae in the Orkney Islands. Here there were few trees, so houses were constructed entirely from stone. Even the beds and cupboards were built from stone. They were partly underground for protection against the cold and were linked by narrow passageways. Six houses built in 3100 BC were completely buried in sand by a sudden, violent storm in 2450 BC. Another storm, in AD 1850, uncovered them.

MEGALITHIC MONUMENTS

Some spectacular megalithic monuments from this period are found throughout western Europe and on Malta and Gozo. Megalith means 'huge stone'.

The monuments include large tombs, stone circles and avenues, and single standing stones, sometimes called menhirs. Some tombs, such as the one at West Kennet in Wiltshire, England, were used over many centuries, for burials and possibly in ceremonies for the dead. The stone circles, avenues and menhirs are more mysterious. Many relate to the positions of the Sun, Moon and Sirius the Dogstar, at various times of the year, especially midwinter and midsummer. So they may have

◆ *At Carnac in northwest France, avenues of standing stones stretch for several kilometres. The stones almost certainly have religious significance.*

◆ *The people at Skara Brae gathered driftwood for fires, but made their furniture and tools from stone.*

Stonehenge, on Salisbury Plain in England, is laid out to mark the positions of the midsummer sunrise and the midwinter moonrise. Some of the stones were transported from the mountains of Wales.

been used as vast outdoor calendars. The Sun was probably important in religious beliefs at this time, as it enabled farmers to predict the seasons.

Many of the megalithic monuments are older than the pyramids in Egypt. As the people who built them had no written language, we have to rely on archaeology to tell us how they were built.

Some monuments were built from local stone, but even this had to be quarried, cut into the right shape and then placed upright in the soil, using only simple tools made from stone, bone or wood. Other stones were transported over long distances, probably by a system of sledges, rollers and ropes. This involved large numbers of people, which suggests that society was very well organized at this time, but we know nothing about its rulers.

◆ The people who lived at Skara Brae may have played games in their spare time. Archaeologists have discovered a pair of dice, carved from bone, at the site.

Bone dice from Skara Brae

◆ From around 4500 BC, farming communities around Europe built tombs for their dead from massive stones. Bodies were placed in a room, or chamber, inside the tomb.

Megalithic tomb, Portugal

◆ At Newgrange in Ireland, the entrance to a megalithic tomb is marked with a massive stone, with a carved design of spirals and diamonds.

Stone from tomb, Newgrange, Ireland

THE BRONZE AGE IN EUROPE

2300–700 BC

The Bronze Age in Europe started around 2300 BC, when people were still building megalithic monuments. At first, only a few tools and weapons were made from bronze. By 1200 BC, however, bronze had completely replaced stone and flint, even for everyday objects.

The copper and tin needed to make bronze were not found in all parts of Europe. Bronze items were therefore traded over great distances. Axes from Brittany have been found in Switzerland, and swords from Hungary have been found in Denmark.

FARMERS

With their new bronze tools, people cleared more of the forests which covered Europe at this time, and brought more land into use for farming. This meant that there was more food, and the population began to increase.

◆ Bronze was used to make luxury items, such as this ceremonial helmet, which was decorated with red enamel and made during the 1st century BC.

◆ There were no explosives, so all mining was done with hand tools. Sometimes a fire was lit near the rock face and, when it got hot, cold water was thrown on. This split the rock and made it easier to move. The rock was crushed, and the copper ore which it contained was separated out, rinsed and smelted in furnaces.

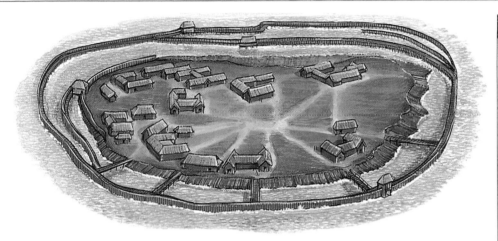

In northwest Europe people still lived in farmsteads and small hamlets, but in the Alps and central and eastern Europe there were bigger settlements. The inhabitants were farmers, but some of the settlements had defensive ditches and palisades, which suggests that the people living there felt threatened by outsiders. From 1250 BC, bronze swords and helmets were made.

◆ Lurer were long Scandinavian trumpets capable of producing a range of twelve or fourteen notes.

◆ Wasserburg was built on an island in the Federsee, in southern Germany, in the 12th century BC. It was protected by a wooden palisade. Its inhabitants kept sheep, pigs, goats, cattle, horses and dogs.

A society based on trade developed in Scandinavia, where neither tin nor copper was mined. To get the bronze items they needed to farm the land, the Scandinavians traded amber, probably together with furs and slaves. They may also have exported cattle and dairy products to central Europe.

Some people were buried with grave goods made from gold and bronze.

This society, however, collapsed in the 8th century BC. The climate had worsened, and trade routes changed, because iron was beginning to replace bronze as the main material for tools and for weapons.

◆ Bronze could be cast in moulds and hammered into shape, and so it could be used to make ornamental axeheads, as well as plain ones for everyday use.

Ornamental axehead, 7th century BC

Coracle made from animal skins stretched over a wooden frame

◆ Much of Europe was heavily forested at this time. Travelling on water was often easier than travelling on land.

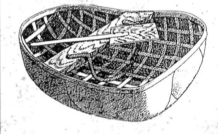

Chariot of the Sun, Denmark

◆ This bronze model chariot was made in Denmark in about 1500 BC. The disc represents the Sun and the Moon. The horse is drawing them on their daily journey across the sky.

THE CELTIC CIVILIZATION

750 BC–AD 500

The ancestors of the people we call the Celts probably lived in parts of France, Germany and the Alps for many generations before a distinctive civilization developed during the early Iron Age. By about 750 BC, there is evidence that they were mining salt at Hallstatt in Austria.

At this time, people could not grow enough crops to feed all their animals over the winter, and so they killed many of them at the end of autumn. The meat then had to last until early summer, and salt was used to preserve it.

◆ Celtic houses were made from local materials. Where trees were plentiful, houses had wooden walls and thatched roofs. If there were not enough trees for this, the walls were built of stone. Inside there was usually just one big room, in which the whole family lived, cooked, ate and slept. Everyone gathered around the fire in the centre, for heat and light.

Many Celts from Hallstatt grew wealthy by taking salt over the mountains and into Greece, where they traded it for other goods. Some of these traded goods were buried with them when they died.

Celtic civilization expanded along the Rhine and Danube Rivers, and by the 6th century BC there were Celtic settlements in France, Spain, Belgium and Britain. Archaeologists call this early part of Celtic civilization, up to about 500 BC, the Hallstatt period, after the village. Next came the La Tène period, named after a site in Switzerland.

THE LA TÈNE PERIOD

During the La Tène period, the Celtic civilization continued to expand, until it had

reached Moravia and Thrace in the east, and Portugal and Ireland in the west. Some Celts even went to Asia Minor and later settled there. The area where they went is still known as Galatia, which comes from 'Gauls', the Roman name for the Celts.

As the Romans became more powerful, they prevented the Celts from expanding their territory farther south. From 225 BC, they beat the Celts in battle, even though the Celts usually had much bigger armies.

The Celts never had an empire. They were made up of many separate tribes, who were often at war with one another if they had no other enemy to fight.

◆ Making bronze mirrors was a specialty of Celtic metalworkers in the 1st century AD.

◆ The Celts used iron for their tools and weapons, but made many finely detailed objects from bronze. These objects often had patterns, based on circles, which were engraved, cut out in filigree or decorated with enamel.

Nevertheless, the Celts were united by their way of life, their language, their arts and crafts and their beliefs.

CELTIC SOCIETY

The Celts left no written records about themselves, but the Romans wrote about them. The Romans considered the Celts to be uncivilized and called them Barbarians. This was probably because the Celtic way of life seemed so different from theirs.

From what the Romans wrote, we know that the Celts divided their society into four main groups. These were made up of nobles, warriors, farmers and learned men. The last group included doctors, bards, metalworkers and priests.

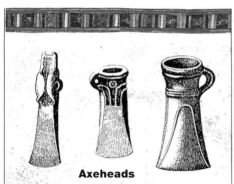

Axeheads

◆ The Celts used axes as tools, rather than as weapons. Different shapes of axehead were used for different jobs.

◆ A gold torc worn around the neck was a symbol of power and rank. Torcs were worn by nobles and warriors, who sometimes went into battle wearing nothing else. They were occasionally worn by noblewomen, too.

Gold torc

◆ Doctors tried their best to heal wounds and other injuries. They sometimes even operated on people's skulls, if they thought an injury was causing a swelling that might damage the brain.

Surgical instruments

◆ The Celts enjoyed drinking alcohol, and wine was a status symbol to them. When they entertained, they sometimes served wine from huge,

Burial krater

decorated containers, called kraters. Often a krater was buried with a rich person when he or she died.

◆ Dice and counters have been found at various Celtic sites around Europe, showing that the Celts enjoyed games of chance. Unfortunately, no rules have survived.

◆ In Ireland the Celts devised a system of writing, known as Ogam or Ogham. It was made up of straight lines, which were easier to carve in stone or wood than curved figures.

Stone showing Irish Celts' system of writing

The Celts had many gods and goddesses, most of whom were connected with nature and the environment. Many were associated with streams, trees and rocks, but in Britain and France there was also a horse goddess called Epona.

Celtic tribes in both these countries had religious leaders known as druids. They were the wise men of the tribe and could take up to 20 years to learn their skills. They demanded sacrifices, sometimes of animals, or even of people, but more often of valuable objects. They also organized the great Celtic festivals of Beltane and Samhain which were important events in the farming year.

In spite of their fierce image, the Celts looked after the poor, the sick and the elderly, and made sure that people were kept warm and well fed.

CELTIC TRADERS
The Celts were farmers and warriors, and also

◆ *Found in the Thames River, at Battersea in London, this bronze shield was too flimsy to have offered much protection in battle. It was probably used in ceremonies only. Its embossed pattern was decorated with red enamel.*

◆ *The hillfort at Maiden Castle in Dorset, England, was defended by a series of banks and ditches. Houses were built on the open area at the top, and the farm animals were brought there to graze in times of danger.*

merchants. They traded their goods, over land and sea, with the Phoenicians, the Greeks and the Romans. From the latter they got wine, olive oil and pottery, in exchange for slaves, woollen cloth and hunting dogs. The traders must have travelled farther still, for one tomb in Germany contained some silk which may have come all the way from China.

Through this trade, the Romans began to realize how rich the Celtic lands were. Their own power continued to increase, and they became determined to make the Celtic lands part of the Roman empire. As Roman generals were to discover, this was no easy task.

The Romans defeated the Celts at the battle of Telamon in 225 BC, and then set out to conquer Gaul. However, their plans were frustrated by the outbreak of war with the Carthaginians, which lasted until 202 BC. After this, they started their conquest again, defeating southern Gaul, Spain and Portugal, before turning back to conquer the rest of Gaul.

They also conquered the Galatians, when Asia Minor in the east became part of the Roman empire.

In many places the Celts became completely Romanized and their old way of life quickly disappeared. Some Celts who were skilled horseriders even joined the Roman cavalry legions and eventually became Roman citizens.

The Romans added Britain to their empire in AD 43, but they never managed to conquer all of it. Scotland and Ireland, together with parts of Wales and Cornwall, remained free from Roman influence, and the Celtic way of life continued there for many more centuries. From the 4th century AD, however, these Celts became Christians and after the collapse of the Roman empire, some of them travelled across to Europe as missionaries.

◆ *At the battle of Alesia in 52 BC, a Roman force of 50,000 soldiers, led by Julius Caesar, defeated almost 350,000 Gauls. Of these, 100,000 were besieged in the oppidum (or fortified settlement) and 250,000 were in a relief force sent to rescue them. The relief force could not break through the Roman defences, so the people in the oppidum were starved into surrendering.*

IN SEARCH OF NEW LANDS

AD 200–600

The Romans tried to extend their empire to the north. Here the Germanic people, whom the Romans also called Barbarians, lived as different tribes, as likely to fight among themselves as against an outside enemy.

Most of the Germanic people were farmers, but some of them were also skilled metalworkers, making beautiful jewellery from gold and coloured stones, as well as tools and weapons. Away from the farms, much of the land was covered in thick forest, an ideal place from which to attack the Romans as they tried to extend their empire beyond the Rhine. The Barbarians prevented them from doing this and in the 2nd century AD they started to attack the Roman frontier in the west.

By the middle of the 3rd century AD, many of the Germanic peoples were on the move, searching for new lands to settle in. The Goths, who were divided into Ostrogoths and Visigoths, and the Vandals moved closer to the borders of the Roman empire. In AD 268, they sacked the city of Athens.

Meanwhile, on the vast plains and steppes to the east of the Roman empire, other peoples were becoming more powerful.

◆ *The Saxons were skilled craftworkers, as is shown by this elaborate helmet, made of bronze, iron and silver. To make the helmet more comfortable to wear, it was lined with leather.*

◆ *Most people could migrate from east to west overland, but the Angles, Jutes and Saxons crossed the North Sea to reach Britain. They travelled in open boats, along with everything they needed to start a new life.*

◆ *The armour men wore in battle may have been ornamental as well as for defence. Both men and women wore jewellery, especially brooches.*

Most lived as nomadic herders, but they were skilled at metalwork and at horse riding. They were also fearless warriors. One of these peoples, the Scythians, were defeated by the Goths in the 3rd century AD. The Goths, in turn, were defeated by the Huns, a Mongolian tribe, in AD 370, and turned to the Roman emperor for protection. The eastern emperor Valens let them settle on his land because he thought they would make useful recruits to his army, but instead they gathered in strength and defeated him.

By AD 400, the Barbarians were on the move all over Europe. Angles,

Jutes and Saxons invaded Britain from across the North Sea, possibly because their own lands had been devastated by flooding. They brought their families with them and settled in the south and east of what was to be named England after the Angles. In AD 417 the Visigoths invaded Gaul, to be followed by the Franks and the Burgundians. The Vandals went to Spain and north Africa. The Huns, led by Attila, reached northern Italy but their power collapsed after his death in 453. The migrations continued for another 100 years.

◆ Drinking vessels were made from cows' horns. The shape made it difficult to put the horn down when there was liquid in it, and so the contents had to be drunk in one go, or passed on.

Drinking vessel

◆ Most of the new settlers were farmers, who chose to live in small communities or individual farmsteads. They built their homes from wood, and let many Roman buildings fall into decay.

Wooden house

◆ Most of the small amount of writing surviving from this period is in stick-like letters known as runes. Poets and storytellers passed on their work by word of mouth.

Runes

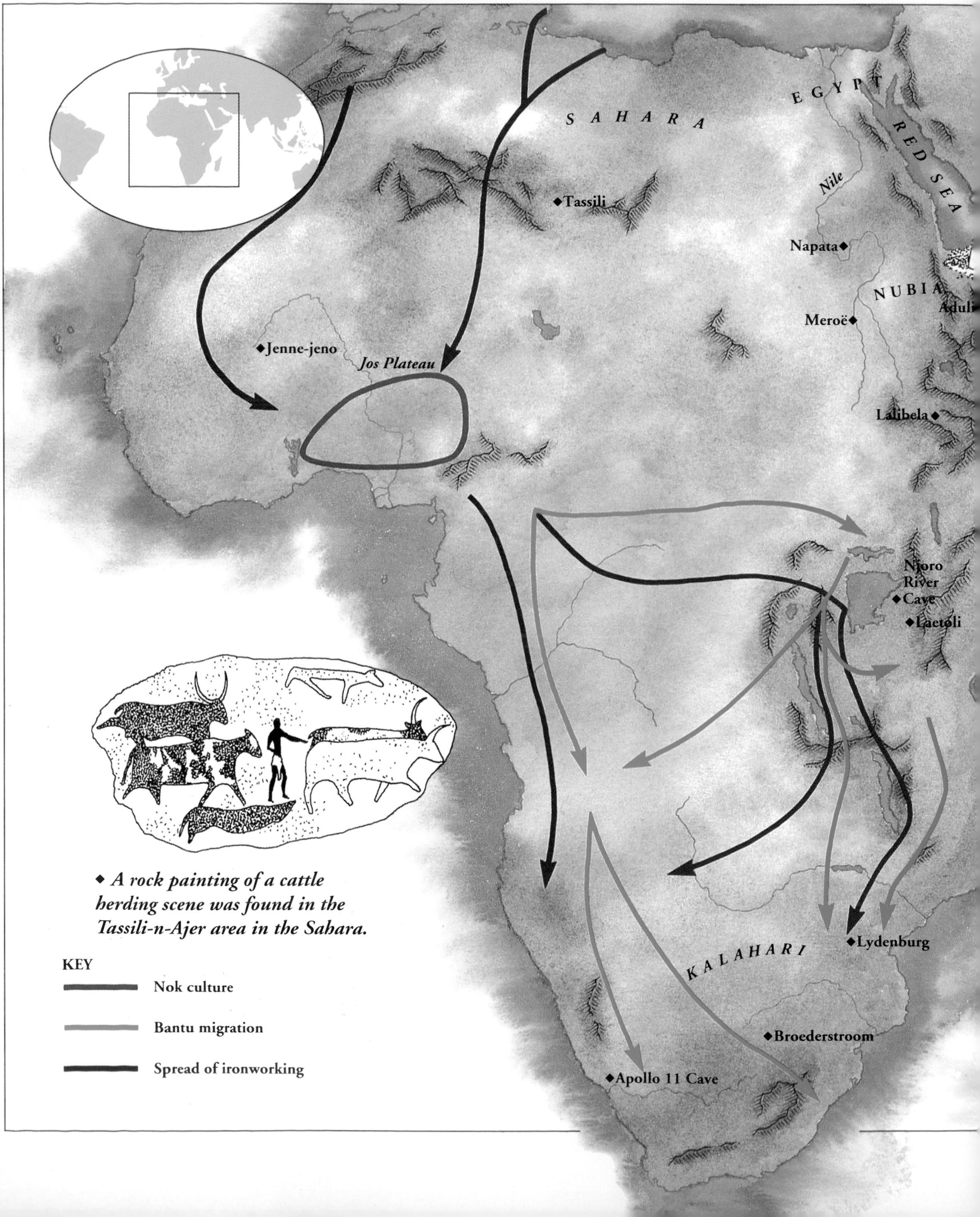

SAHARA

EGYPT

RED SEA

Nile

Tassili

Napata

NUBIA

Meroë

Adul

Jenne-jeno

Jos Plateau

Lalibela

Njoro
River
Cave

Laetoli

♦ *A rock painting of a cattle herding scene was found in the Tassili-n-Ajer area in the Sahara.*

KALAHARI

Lydenburg

Broederstroom

Apollo 11 Cave

KEY

────── Nok culture

────── Bantu migration

────── Spread of ironworking

AFRICA

The first humans lived in the vast grasslands and wooded areas of central Africa. For many thousands of years, as people spread across the continent, they found food by hunting and gathering, using tools made from stone and wood.

No great ice sheets covered Africa during the last Ice Age. There was, however, a problem with drought. In around 20-10,000 BC, the Sahara Desert was larger and drier than today, and no people or animals could live there. When temperatures rose worldwide and water was released from the ice, rains fell again and plants, animals and people moved back into the Sahara.

Farther south, people continued to live by hunting and gathering for many centuries. Some tools, weapons, pots and traces of post holes and fires are the only evidence of their existence.

• **The north cemetery of Meroë. The pyramids were made from sandstone.**

• **A terracotta head found at Lydenburg, Transvaal. It was made around AD 500.**

MADAGASCAR

THE FIRST FARMERS OF AFRICA

9000–2000 BC

By 9000 BC, enough water had been released from the ice sheets for rain to fall again. Conditions in the Sahara improved to the extent that groups of people moved back there from north and south. Grasslands grew around the edges of the desert, and scrubby woodland grew on high ground. This attracted wildlife back into the area. Rock carvings and paintings from around 8500 BC show giraffes, elephants, hippopotamuses and rhino-ceroses. These animals were all hunted for their meat and skins.

By 6000 BC, the desert was probably at its smallest, and conditions were wet enough for lakes to form in some places. A rock painting from this time even shows hunters trying to spear a hippo from a canoe.

FROM HUNTING TO FARMING

Other rock paintings from around 6000 BC show people herding cattle, rather than hunting them. This move from hunting to farming is confirmed by archaeologists' finds of domesticated cattle bones at several different sites in the Sahara, dated to between 6500 and 4000 BC. According to the paintings, people also tried, without success, to domesticate other animals, including giraffes.

As well as grazing for animals, the grasslands provided plants which were suitable for humans to eat. For example, both millet and sorghum produced grain. At first, people harvested them from the wild, using sickles made from wood and flint,

◆ *The paintings and engravings on the rocks at Tassili have been dated to around 3000 BC. The paint was made by crushing rocks and soils of different colours and mixing them with melted animal fat.*

◆ *As the Sahara began to dry out, cattle herders were forced to keep moving their cattle around from one oasis to another, in search of water.*

but by 6000 BC these plants were being cultivated.

By this time, people lived in permanent settlements by the rivers and lakes of the Sahara, and in the grasslands to the south. They ate hippos and crocodiles, as well as fish. They decorated their pottery with wavy lines.

THE DESERT EXPANDS AGAIN

In around 4000 BC, another dry period started. The lakes began to disappear and the grasslands to wither. Animals either migrated or became extinct. Rock art from after 3000 BC shows camels and other animals more suited to desert conditions. As the desert expanded, people moved out or followed a nomadic life in search of water for themselves and their cattle.

By 2000 BC, the Sahara had grown to about the size it is today. It separated the Mediterranean coast of north Africa from the rest of the continent. Only trade routes remained open through the desert, and the two parts of Africa began to develop in quite different ways.

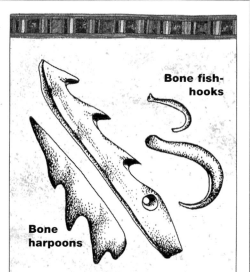

Bone fish-hooks

Bone harpoons

◆ Even after people started farming, they still needed to hunt some of their food. They fished with harpoons, fish-hooks and spears, and used bows and arrows to kill animals on land. The stone arrowheads were fixed in place with mastic, which was a natural gum.

◆ Millet, sorghum and yams were among the first crops cultivated in Africa. Millet became especially important as the land dried out, because it does not need as much moisture as sorghum.

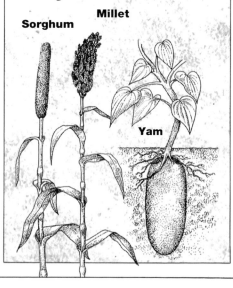

Sorghum

Millet

Yam

NUBIA AND THE KINGDOM OF KUSH

2000 BC–AD 400

◆ *A wall painting from an Egyptian tomb shows Nubians bringing the pharaoh gifts of fruit, gold jewellery, furs, cloth and monkeys.*

Nubia was on the Nile River, just south of Egypt. Although it was surrounded by desert, the land alongside the river was kept fertile by the annual floods. Tomb paintings from Egypt show that the Nubians were black Africans, and written references often describe them as tall and strong.

Egyptian civilization reached Nubia by about 2000 BC, which was also when the kingdom of Kush was starting to develop there. Its capital was at Napata, just below the fourth cataract on the Nile. Soon trade was flourishing, with the Nubians supplying Egypt with gold, ivory, exotic animals and fruits. Nubians also joined the Egyptian army as mercenaries.

By the 15th century BC, an Egyptian viceroy ruled over Nubia. As Egypt's power declined towards the end of the New Kingdom period, however, that of Kush began to increase.

By around 750 BC, the Kushite army defeated the Egyptians at Memphis, and the Kushite rulers founded the 25th dynasty of pharaohs. It lasted until 663 BC, when the Egyptians were conquered by the Assyrians and the Kushite rulers returned to the lands of Nubia and their capital at Napata.

IRONWORKING BRINGS WEALTH
In about 600 BC, they changed their capital to Meroë, farther south on the Nile. Knowledge of ironworking had spread from Egypt and, as Meroë was surrounded by deposits of iron ore, it quickly grew in size and wealth. By 500 BC it had grown into a city of mudbrick houses built around cemeteries of pyramid-like tombs, which in turn were built around a complex of royal temples. The most important one at this time

◆ *Even after Nubia became independent again, Egyptian influence remained strong. For example, in Meroë, kings and queens were buried in Egyptian-style pyramids, although they were slightly taller and narrower than Egyptian ones. Greek and Roman influence later filtered down from Egypt, but was never as strong as that of Egypt.*

was dedicated to Amun, the Egyptian Sun god, but later ones were dedicated to the Nubians' own gods, such as Marduk.

Meroë had trade links with the Mediterranean via the Nile, while camel trains brought goods from Arabia overland from Red Sea ports.

As Egyptian influence declined, the Nubians used an alphabetical script in place of hieroglyphs. It has been deciphered, but the language has not yet been translated.

Nubia and Kush remained independent, even after Egypt was conquered by the Romans in 30 BC. But by AD 400 their power was waning.

♦ On scaffolding high above Napata, workers carved hieroglyphs in the rock. The hieroglyphs commemorated Kushite kings and were covered with a sheet of gold that gleamed in the sun.

♦ Wall paintings in Egypt show that both Nubian men and women wore tight-fitting necklaces made from animal teeth of different sizes.

Nubian necklace

♦ The Lion Temple at Naga in Nubia was built by King Natekamani and Queen Amantare around AD 1. By this time Egypt itself was part of the Roman empire, but the influence of earlier Egyptian building styles was still strong in Nubia and this temple copied them. It was dedicated to Apemedek, the lion god, and his image appears on carvings.

The Lion Temple at Naga

♦ As the kingdom of Kush declined in power after AD 400, the Nubian kingdoms were converted to Christianity by missionary monks from the eastern Roman empire of Byzantium.

NOK CULTURE AND BANTU SPEAKERS

400 BC–AD 500

In around 400 BC, knowledge of ironworking reached the Nok people in what is now northern Nigeria. It was brought there possibly from the area around Meroë in the kingdom of Kush, or perhaps from the Mediterranean coast, by traders crossing the Sahara Desert.

♦ *In places such as the rainforest and the Kalahari Desert, where the Bantu did not settle, the people continued their traditional way of life until the 20th century.*

Since 1800 BC, people in this part of west Africa had lived in village communities of farmers. Archaeological evidence in Ghana shows that their houses were rectangular, with wattle and daub walls and thatched roofs. The people kept goats and cattle, and grew oil palms and yams. Their tools and weapons were made from stone, bone or wood. These were not very effective, and so farming took place on a small scale.

THE ADVANTAGES OF IRON

Once iron was introduced, however, the Nok people could farm more successfully. Iron tools were stronger, more efficient, and easier to replace. With iron-headed axes, the people cleared more land for farming, by felling trees and clearing undergrowth. They probably used some timber for building and fuel, but they burned the rest where it had fallen, just before the rainy season. Then they hoed the ash into the ground, to give some goodness back to the soil, before preparing it with digging sticks for planting.

These advances in farming allowed the Nok culture to flourish between 400 BC and AD 200. Some people became skilled sculptors.

◆ *Most of the terracotta figures made by the Nok were of human heads. Many of them are life-size and show details of hairstyles and jewellery.*

BANTU SPEAKERS

In the 1st century AD, a new group of people from west Africa joined those living just south of the land of the Nok. The new-comers spoke languages derived from Bantu, and they were farmers. Eventually, they began to move south and east across the continent, in search of new lands to settle in. They took with them the knowledge they had gained of farming and ironworking, and introduced these in places which had previously been occupied only by hunter-gatherers.

By AD 500, the newcomers had reached southern Africa, where they lived in small villages. They cultivated cereal crops and kept herds of sheep, cattle and goats, as well as smelting iron and making pottery. They settled only in places which were suitable for the farming techniques of the time, however. This meant that they left the rainforest to the Pygmies, and the Kalahari Desert to the Bushmen.

◆ *The iron ore was smelted in two different types of clay furnaces. One was dome-shaped and the other was like a cylinder, with a pit underneath to catch the molten metal as it ran out of the ore. Both types of furnace had a series of clay pipes, called* tuyères, *built into the walls at the level of the fire. Bellows could be used to force air through the* tuyères, *to make the fire hotter.*

◆ As well as using pottery, people in Africa carved bowls and other containers from wood. This finely decorated example dates from the 12th century BC, and was found at Njoro River Cave in Kenya.

Wooden bowl, Kenya

◆ Iron tools made at this time included axeheads and hoes, knives, arrowheads and spearheads. They made people more effective as hunters and farmers.

Wooden house, Transvaal

◆ In the 5th century AD, the people of Broederstroom in the Transvaal lived in dome-shaped houses. The wooden framework was covered with mats of plaited grass and then plastered inside and out with clay. The floor was made in the same way, and rested on timber beams supported by large stones.

THE KINGDOM OF AXUM

500 BC–AD 600

The kingdom of Axum, in what is now Ethiopia, began its rise to power in the first millennium BC. Its wealth was built on trade, through its main port at Adulis on the Red Sea.

At first Axum was strongly influenced by southern Arabia, and in the 5th century BC its language and writing bore a close relationship to Arabic. From the 4th century, however, Greek influence became more important, as traders from Ptolemaic Egypt passed through Adulis on their way to India. The main goods traded at this time were probably ivory, gold, precious stones, wine and slaves. Monkeys and other animals were caught and traded live as pets and some elephants were also caught and trained to work.

A TRADERS' MEETING PLACE

Early in the 1st century AD, two things happened which increased Axum's strength and wealth. A new line of strong rulers came to power there, with a king of kings ruling from Axum and several less important kings ruling over smaller areas and paying a yearly tax or tribute to the king of kings. At the same time, people developed a new understanding of the monsoon wind system. Sailors were able to work out how to take advantage of the winds, to make travel easier between the Mediterranean and the Indian Ocean, via the Red Sea. Silk from China began to travel along this route, as well as continuing to travel overland.

It was rare to do the whole of the sea journey on the same ship,

♦ *Axumite traders and merchants bought and sold luxury goods from all parts of the world as it was then known: ivory from Africa, wine from Rome, myrrh and frankincense from Arabia, fine silks, brocades and lacquerware from China, and spices from India.*

The early Christian churches were cut into solid rock. The one at Lalibela in Ethiopia is in the shape of a cross.

and so many traders and merchants stopped off on their way, at the Axumite port of Adulis. Even traders of frankincense and myrrh, who had previously travelled overland from southern Arabia to the Mediterranean, began to travel through Adulis, as did spice merchants from India. Spices were an essential commodity at a time when there were no refrigerators to keep food fresh, as they helped to hide the taste of meat which was beginning to go bad. Frankincense was needed for religious ceremonies and for embalming, while myrrh was used in perfumes, cosmetics and medicine.

In the 4th century AD, Christianity also came to Axum along the trade routes from the Mediterranean, and remained the main religion in Ethiopia into the 20th century. Also in the 4th century, skilled stonemasons erected huge granite *stelae* or obelisks, as a sign of their country's growing wealth and power. Some stelae are carved with the symbols of the pre-Christian gods. They include Hawbas the Moon god and Mahrem who was the god of war and kings. Ancestors were also worshipped and animals sacrificed to them.

By the 6th century, Axum was so powerful that it took control of the Incense States of western Arabia. These were the main growers of frankincense and myrrh.

♦ *This obelisk commemorating one of the Axumite rulers is still standing today. It is 30 metres high, but it has started to lean.*

♦ Ships sailing from Axum were able to take advantage of the monsoon wind system to reach India and bring goods back from there. The sailors realized that in winter the winds blew from the northeast, helping them to sail to India, while in the summer the winds changed direction, helping them to sail back. The goods they bought probably included valuable jewels as well as spices.

Palace at Enda Mikael

♦ Axumite rulers used some of their wealth to build themselves fine palaces. The palace at Enda Mikael measured 27 metres along each side and had battlements on the tower at each corner.

♦ Gold coins made after Axum became Christian had a cross on them, as well as the head of the ruler. This emperor, Ousanas, ruled from AD 285 to 317.

Gold coin

THE AMERICAS

During the last Ice Age, as the sea level fell, a land bridge slowly appeared between Asia and North America. Eventually, it was 1600 kilometres wide. It is known as Beringia.

Both animals and hunters crossed from Asia to a continent where no human beings had lived before. When the ice melted and the sea level began to rise again, the American continent was cut off once more from the rest of the world, and its own diverse civilizations developed, influenced by their natural surroundings. Some peoples were nomadic, following herds around the countryside, while others settled and developed farms.

There were strong trade links among the various civilizations. Villages, towns and cities developed, and some of these had fine stone buildings.

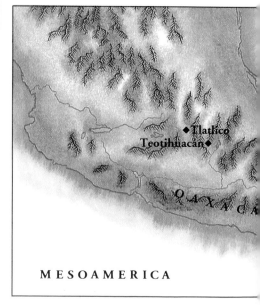

MESOAMERICA

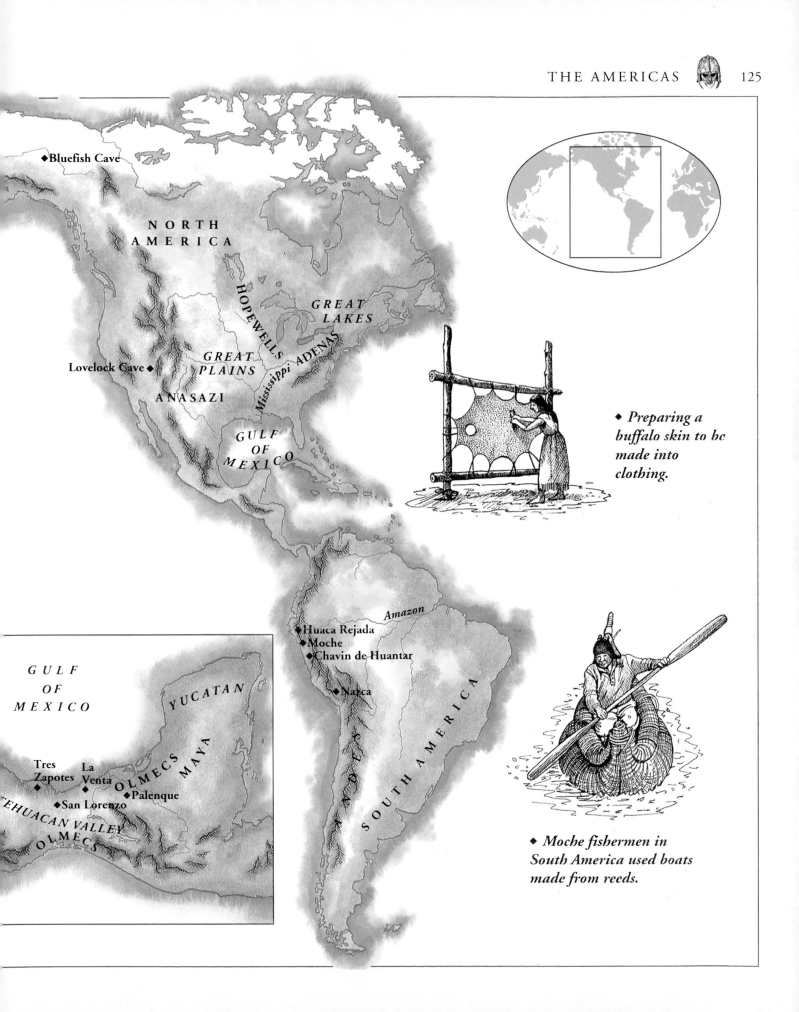

◆ Bluefish Cave

NORTH
AMERICA

HOPEWELLS

GREAT
LAKES

GREAT
PLAINS

Lovelock Cave ◆

ANASAZI

Mississippi ADENAS

GULF
OF
MEXICO

Amazon

◆ Huaca Rejada
◆ Moche
◆ Chavin de Huantar

◆ Nazca

ANDES

SOUTH AMERICA

GULF
OF
MEXICO

YUCATAN

MAYA

OLMECS

Tres
Zapotes
◆

La
Venta
◆

◆ Palenque

◆ San Lorenzo

TEHUACAN VALLEY

OLMECS

◆ *Preparing a
buffalo skin to be
made into
clothing.*

◆ *Moche fishermen in
South America used boats
made from reeds.*

THE EARLY SETTLERS IN NORTH AMERICA

35,000 BC–AD 600

As the ice sheets began to melt, the animals that had crossed the land bridge from Siberia, and the hunters and their families who had crossed with them, started to head south and east. Eventually, they reached all parts of the continent that is now Canada and the United States.

At first, the people lived a nomadic life, hunting the large animals that had flourished during the Ice Age, such as the mammoth, the mastodon and the long-horned bison.

All tools were made from stone, wood or bone, and included knives, scrapers and hammers, which were used to butcher the animals after they had been killed. The main hunting weapon was a spear, with a wooden handle and a stone point fixed in at one end and bound into place with thongs made of animal skin.

NEW ANIMALS

Between 10,000 BC and 4000 BC, the Earth's climate warmed up again and the water which had been locked up in the ice circulated freely once more. Great changes occurred in climate and environment, and this led to the extinction of most of the big animals, including the horse, by about 8000 BC.

That date marks the end of what is known as the Palaeo-Indian period. During the Archaic period,

◆ *People hunted large herds of animals for food. For example, archaeological evidence in Colorado suggests that, in about 6500 BC, a herd of bison was chased until they stampeded over a cliff and fell to their deaths.*

which lasted from 8000 BC to 1000 BC, the large animals were replaced by smaller ones, such as antelope, deer and caribou. People began to follow more varied ways of life, depending on where they lived and the resources available to them.

LIVING IN THE ARCTIC

In the Arctic regions people killed walruses for their meat, and also used their ivory tusks to make tools. Sealskins were turned into warm clothing.

◆ *People who settled in the river valleys in southeastern North America built their houses from a framework of wooden poles covered with thatch. They were roughly circular, and could house up to 20 people.*

Tube and pipe, Tennessee

♦ A tube and pipe, carved in the shape of a bear's head, were found in what is now Tennessee. They may have been used for smoking in some kind of ceremony, although tobacco was not used at this time. They may also have had something to do with healing the sick.

♦ Different stone points were used to kill different types of animal. The Folsom point, shown here, was used to kill bison. For skinning mammoths, the Clovis point was about half as long again.

Folsom point

♦ In the far north, hunters used carved counterbalances on the butt end of their harpoons. They thought that the beauty of their weapons would please the spirits of the animals and make them easier to catch.

Harpoon ornament

In the depths of winter, people built shelters from blocks of frozen snow. For the brief summer period, they may have made tents, from wooden poles and skins.

THE SUBARCTIC AND THE GREAT PLAINS

In the Subarctic zone hunters followed the great herds of caribou which migrated to find food, and then settled permanently farther south in areas where the temperature became warmer and they could find food more easily.

On the Great Plains, too, people still led a nomadic life, following the herds of bison. Often they killed and butchered several at a time and then preserved the meat by drying it in long strips, to make pemmican. They used the bison skins for clothes and shelter. The way of life of these people continued almost unchanged until the Spanish reintroduced horses around AD 1500.

Walrus ivory harpoon points

◆ Harpoons with walrus-ivory points were used for catching large fish and sea mammals. Small fish could be speared in shallow water. In deeper water they were caught on bone hooks suspended from lengths of twine. Nets were also used in some places, and some fish were caught in basketwork traps set into rivers and streams.

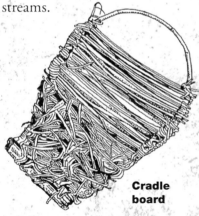

Cradle board

◆ The people who lived on the edge of the deserts of the southwest carried their babies in flexible cradle boards. At first, the boards were padded with juniper bark or hide, to protect the baby's head. After AD 700, a hard board was used to make the back of the baby's skull grow flat, as this was thought to be a sign of beauty.

In some areas where there were more resources, people began to settle. Hunting was still important, but they also gathered seeds, nuts and berries, to add to their diet. New tools and utensils began to appear, including nets and snares for catching smaller animals and birds, fish-hooks and weighted fishing-lines, baskets for gathering and storing, and *metates* (stones) for crushing and grinding nuts and seeds.

In other areas, by contrast, people began to think about growing crops, in order to ensure their food supply. The adoption of agriculture, from around 1000 BC, marks the start of what is called the Formative period. During this time, many distinct cultures began to develop. None of them had a written language, and, unfortunately, much

archaeological evidence was destroyed, either accidentally or on purpose, by migrants to North America in the 18th and 19th centuries. Many aspects of Native American life can only be

◆ *Fortunately some of the burial mounds left behind by the Native Americans were discovered by archaeologists in the 19th century. They excavated them carefully and made detailed paintings and drawings of what they found.*

◆ *The Hopewells and the Adenas built large earthworks in Ohio and Kentucky. Many were square or circular, but some were shaped like animals. The Great Serpent Mound is 390 metres long, but 500 metres if all the twists are taken into account.*

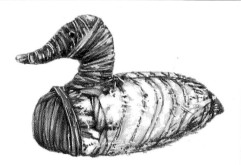

◆ *This decoy duck made from reeds was found in Lovelock Cave, Nevada. It would have been covered in feathered birdskin, to make it look more realistic.*

guessed at. Nonetheless, we do know a good deal about two groups of people.

THE ANASAZI

The Anasazi lived in the semi-arid high plateau country of Arizona, New Mexico, Utah and Colorado. They built their homes partly underground, and sometimes protected by an overhanging cliff. In summer, they wore very little other than woven sandals to protect their feet from thorns. In winter, they had cloaks made from rabbit skin and feathers.

The Anasazi built dams to conserve what little water there was, and planted maize, beans and squash in the mud which formed in dammed-up areas. They added to their diet by gathering nuts, seeds and berries from the wild and by hunting wild animals. Large animals, such as deer, were probably roasted, but small animals were stewed in a pot over the fire with cereals and vegetables. Archaeological evidence shows that even animals as small as mice were sometimes eaten.

THE HOPEWELLS

Living in an area that stretched from the Great Lakes in the north to the mouth of the Mississippi River, the Hopewells grew maize, beans and sunflowers in garden plots alongside their houses, which were usually grouped in villages.

The Hopewells traded goods, including pottery, throughout their territory. They also built temple mounds, and buried some of their dead with grave goods, which they thought they might need for the next life.

Eagle's claw

Bird

◆ *Trade was important to the Hopewells. Pendants made from shells from the Gulf of Mexico have been found in settlements by the Great Lakes. These may have been exchanged for other decorative artefacts (above).*

MESOAMERICA UP TO THE OLMECS

7000–400 BC

The first people in Mesoamerica lived by hunting, and there is evidence that as late as 8000 BC they killed mammoths by driving them into marshy ground and spearing them. By this time, however, changes in climate had led to the extinction of most animals that had lived in Mesoamerica during the Ice Age, and people were relying more on plants for their food. Maize, beans, squash, avocados, chilli peppers and gourds had been domesticated by 5000 BC, and were becoming a main part of people's diets.

At first, people lived in cave mouths during the coldest periods of the year, but by 2000 BC they started to build houses, grouped together in small villages surrounded by fields of crops. Their diet became more varied, with fruits and nuts. They kept bees for honey, and domesticated wild turkeys and ducks for meat. Eventually, they made pottery, spun yarn and wove cloth. By 1150 BC, the people in the valley of Oaxaca lived in large villages. They buried mirrors, shell ornaments, ear spools and pottery in the graves of the rich. Just to the north of the valley of Oaxaca, another distinguishable civilization was developing.

◆ Pyramids with a temple on top were the centre of Olmec religious worship.

◆ Olmec pyramids were built by hand, from earth and clay. It is estimated that it took the equivalent of 800,000 working days to complete the pyramid at La Venta.

◆ Unlike Europe, Asia and Africa, Mesoamerica had no large animals which could be tamed and used for their meat. Therefore it was essential to grow crops for food. Cotton was also cultivated, and made into cloth.

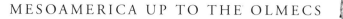

THE OLMECS

The Olmec culture developed in around 1200 BC, in a small area on the Gulf of Mexico. Harpy eagles, caimans and snakes lived in the tropical jungle here, and the Olmec gods were based on these animals and on the sacred jaguar. They influenced later gods throughout Mesoamerica.

Much of our knowledge of the Olmecs comes from their religious ceremonial centres, such as San Lorenzo, La Venta and Tres Zapotes. Each had a pyramid with a temple on top, and sculptures and carvings of gods and rulers.

The economy was based on farming and agriculture, with maize being the main crop. Fish and dogs were eaten, as were deer and wild pigs.

The Olmecs set up trade routes to obtain the stones basalt, obsidian and jade, and their influence spread along these routes. In around 400 BC, however, the site of La Venta was abandoned and the Olmecs' importance declined.

◆ *The Olmecs carved huge heads out of the volcanic rock, basalt. These were up to three metres high, and probably represented different rulers. All the heads were shown wearing a helmet, similar to those worn in the Olmecs' sacred ball game.*

◆ One of the Olmec gods was the were-jaguar, a mixture of human and animal. It was always shown on carvings with fangs and a snarling, down-turned mouth.

Stone carving of the were-jaguar

◆ As well as carving figures out of solid blocks of stone, the Olmecs also made them out of pottery. Many of the pottery figures were hollow and could be used for storing liquids. This one was found at Tlatlico, which is many kilometres from the Olmecs' homeland.

Hollow pottery figure found at Tlatilco

◆ The Olmecs' homeland only covered an area of about 200 kilometres long and 50 kilometres wide. In spite of this, Olmec influence reached as far as the Valley of Mexico.

◆ The Olmecs had a system of writing which used hieroglyphs. Some of these are known from a stone stele found at Tres Zapotes.

THE CITY OF TEOTIHUACAN

150 BC–AD 600

People had settled on the site of Teotihuacán, in the Valley of Mexico, by 150 BC, but it developed as a city only in the 1st century AD. It grew up around a cave which had religious significance for early farmers in the area: they believed it was the place where the Sun and Moon were born. The cave was eventually incorporated into the Pyramid of the Sun, which stood in the ceremonial centre of Teotihuacán.

The city centre was carefully laid out. The Avenue of the Dead ran north to south and was crossed by another avenue running east to west. Where the avenues met, there was the Great Compound, which was probably the main marketplace, and the Cuidadela, where the rulers probably lived in palaces.

The rest of the city covered over 20 square kilometres and was laid out in a grid pattern. People were persuaded to move in from the surrounding countryside, and by AD 500 Teotihuacán's population was about 200,000. The poorest homes were adobe huts, but most craftworkers, farmers and traders lived with their families in single-storey compounds of rooms around courtyards.

◆ *The walls of some temples at Teotihuacán were decorated with carved stone heads.*

THE PEOPLE AT WORK

Workshops produced pottery, obsidian tools and weapons, carved shells, and polished stones, such as onyx and jade. These goods were traded for white jade, flint and haematite from the north, sea shells from the Pacific coast, copal (a

◆ *The nobility in Teotihuacán wore a nose pendant and ear spools, such as appear on this mask.*

kind of sweet-smelling incense) from the Gulf of Mexico and the green feathers from the quetzal bird from the Mayans.

The people irrigated the land in the Teotihuacán Valley and grew crops. They took salt, fish and waterfowl from the nearby lakes, and quarried stone.

The only surviving written evidence about Teotihuacán comes from dates on calendars: no documents survive. We do not know how it was ruled, or why it was destroyed by fire in around AD 750.

◆ *The Pyramid of the Moon stood at the north end of the Avenue of the Dead, with the huge Pyramid of the Sun nearby. The Avenue was more than five kilometres long.*

◆ Obsidian was brought to Teotihuacán from the volcanic hills in the north and east. It was ground and polished into razor-sharp tools.

Obsidian scraper and arrowhead

◆ The people of Teotihuacán made great use of the manguey cactus, which they grew as a crop. They spun the fibres from its leaves into thread, which could be woven into cloth. They also made an intoxicating drink from it.

Tlaloc

◆ The Teotihuacán gods included Tlaloc, the god of rain, his consort, Chalchihuitlicue, who was the rain goddess, and Quetzalcoatl, the feathered serpent. This pottery stamp shows Tlaloc wearing an elaborate headdress.

THE MAYA CIVILIZATION

300 BC–AD 600

As long ago as 2000 BC, the Maya lived in the jungles of what we now call Yucatán, Guatemala, Belize and Honduras. Their civilization developed fully from about 300 BC, when they started to build cities out of stone.

The cities were all independent states, with no overall ruler. They were also built without any defences, which at first led archaeologists and historians to believe that the Maya were peaceful people. But when their system of writing was deciphered in the 1950s, it was clear that they were warlike and often fought against one another. The victors demanded tribute from the defeated and also took prisoners.

Each city was a political and religious centre, built around a complex of temples, plazas, ball courts and palaces. Some of the remains show Teotihuacán influence, such as temples on top of huge platforms in the shape of pyramids.

The cities had populations of up to 50,000 people, made up of nobles, priests, rulers, officials and their servants. Everyone else lived on their farms, where they grew maize, chilli peppers, beans, squash and root crops. They came into the cities only for market days or religious festivals.

CRAFTWORKERS AND TRADE

A network of roads through the jungles encouraged trade, between the cities and beyond the Maya frontiers, too. Some

◆ *Most Mayas were farmers living in small villages. They grew crops and varied their diet by catching fish in basketwork traps and by hunting animals, such as deer, in the surrounding forests.*

goods came by sea to ports on the Yucatán coast.

Craftworkers made beads, pendants and small figures from jade. They carved shell, stone and obsidian, and made pots from long coils of clay. Wallpaintings decorated the tombs and temples.

RELIGION

The Maya worshipped natural things, such as the wind and rain. From

◆ Many Maya cities developed in areas cleared of thick jungle. Once the cities were abandoned, the jungle grew back and hid their ruins, and so many have survived to this day.

observations of the Sun, Moon, stars and planets, their priests worked out a calendar, which showed when eclipses would occur. They also worked out a system of arithmetic based on the number 20, using only three symbols. These were a dot for each number up to four, a bar for the number five, and a shell for zero.

The religion sometimes demanded sacrifices, and defeated enemies who had been taken prisoner were usually sacrificed at religious festivals.

◆ Maya men played a ball game on large courtyards in front of their temples. They hit the solid ball with their elbows, thighs or hips.

Ball-game marker

◆ This marker was used to divide up the court, ready for the sacred ball game. We do not know the rules, but we do know that one of the teams was sometimes sacrificed.

◆ Maya hieroglyphs were both carved onto huge stone monuments and written with a kind of ink in books made from bark paper. Some were used as emblems for cities and rulers.

◆ The temple at Palenque was one of the main ceremonial centres for the Maya. Priests or officials, as represented in this stone carving, prayed to the gods and celebrated various rituals. They may also have made human sacrifices.

Stone carving of a priest or official

SOUTH AMERICAN CIVILIZATIONS

1200 BC–AD 600

Some of the earliest settlements in South America were along the coast of northern Peru. These farming communities grew maize, peppers, beans and sweet potatoes, and added to their diet by hunting. Possibly they kept small herds of llama and alpaca.

From around 1200 BC, a more sophisticated culture appeared farther inland. It is called the Chavin culture, after Chavin de Huantar, the site where it was discovered. This civilization was also based on farming, fishing and hunting.

The town of Chavin de Huantar was at its peak between 850 BC and 200 BC. It was centred on a temple complex, built on top of a stone mound. Inside the mound were passages and rooms, some containing carvings of Chavin gods. The biggest was the Great Image which stood 4.5 metres high. It had huge fangs and snakes in its hair. Other gods sometimes took half-human, half-animal form, and so images of jaguars, eagles, snakes and caimans also appear.

Craftworkers used these images to decorate pottery and other artefacts made from wood, shells, gold and silver. The images were also woven into or painted onto wool and cotton cloth.

◆ *The graves of two Moche warrior-priests were discovered in a complex of pyramids at Huaca Rejada in 1987.*

◆ *A Moche vase, showing how men looked and dressed. Moche pottery is very varied and gives us information about the culture, such as the kind of houses people lived in.*

◆ *A Chavin sculptor carved this bowl from a stone and made it into the shape of an animal. The body and face were decorated with geometric swirls and patterns.*

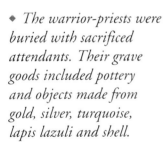

Chavin influence declined after about 200 BC, and two more civilizations developed.

THE NAZCA AND THE MOCHE

To the south, the Nazca created mysterious images in the landscape, and also made textiles and painted pottery.

In the north, the Moche used adobe building material to build towns and religious centres. The Pyramid of the Sun was 350 metres long and 40 metres high. They irrigated the desert, so as to produce more crops, and they expanded their territory by military conquest. For all this, however, by AD 600 Moche and Nazca power was in decline.

◆ *The warrior-priests were buried with sacrificed attendants. Their grave goods included pottery and objects made from gold, silver, turquoise, lapis lazuli and shell.*

◆ *The Nazca created enormous outlines of figures in the desert landscape of Peru, including a monkey, a spider, a killer whale and a hummingbird. Their purpose is a mystery.*

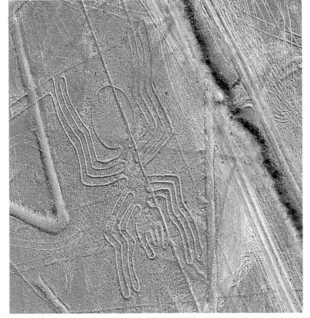

Mosaic figure on ear spool

◆ Ear spools were a popular form of jewellery in this part of South America. They were worn by some of the men, who also wore nose-ornaments, necklaces and bracelets. The figure above is a mosaic set in a round ear spool. It is slightly larger than actual size, which shows how skilled the metal-workers of the time were. The mosaic is made from pieces of gold, semi-precious stones and shell.

◆ The llama was an extremely useful animal. It gave milk and meat, as well as wool and hide. It could also be used as a beast of burden. Its fat was used as oil in lamps and its dung was burned as fuel, or used to fertilize potato crops.

◆ Nazca pottery was often decorated with fierce-looking characters with their tongues sticking out. The Strangler, shown here, was a character in local mythology.

Nazca bowl

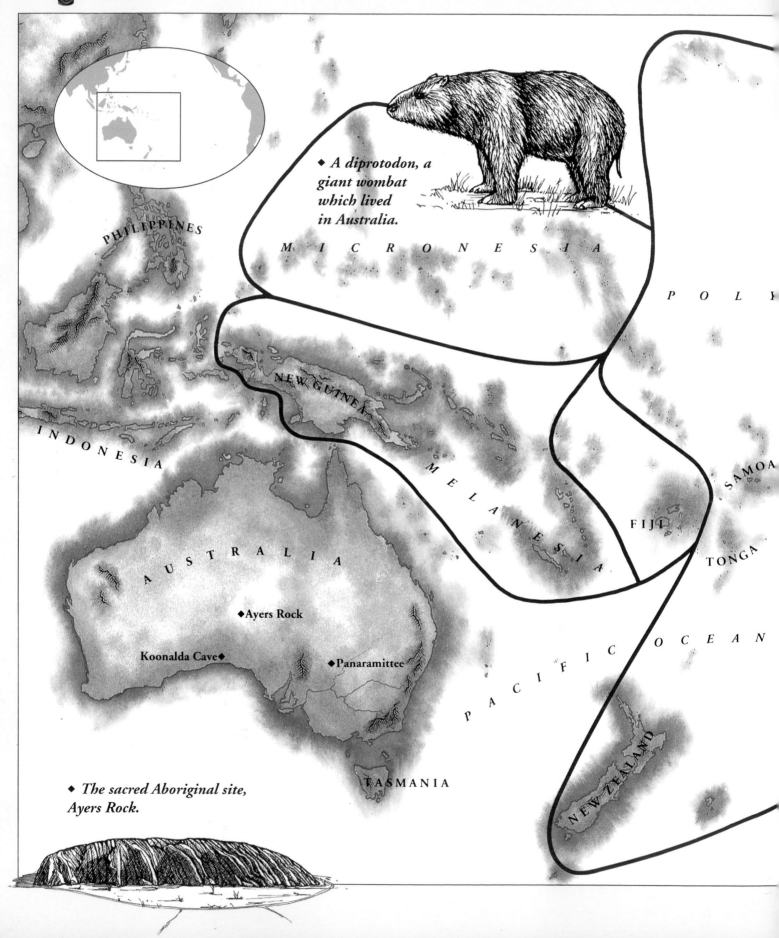

PHILIPPINES

M I C R O N E S I A

◆ *A diprotodon, a giant wombat which lived in Australia.*

INDONESIA

NEW GUINEA

P O L Y

M E L A N E S I A

SAMOA

FIJI

TONGA

A U S T R A L I A

◆Ayers Rock

Koonalda Cave◆

◆Panaramittee

P A C I F I C   O C E A N

TASMANIA

NEW ZEALAND

◆ *The sacred Aboriginal site, Ayers Rock.*

HAWAII

NESIA

OCEANIA

As its name suggests, Oceania is mostly ocean. Many groups of islands are scattered across it. But during an Ice Age 55,000 years ago there were two large land masses. The northern one joined the islands of Japan to the east coast of China, on past Korea and Indo-China to include Sumatra, Java, Borneo and the Philippines. The southern one surrounded Australia and linked it to Tasmania and New Guinea.

When these land masses were at their greatest, the longest sea crossing between southeast Asia and Australia would have been 60 kilometres. Although difficult, it would have been possible to make this journey in a sturdy canoe or raft, and this is probably how the first people arrived in Australia and started to settle there.

It was about AD 400 before most of the islands were settled, and about AD 800 before people settled in New Zealand.

♦ *A representation of the Polynesian god Tangaroa Upao Vahu.*

THE ABORIGINES OF AUSTRALIA

53,000 BC–AD 600

The first people who went from southeast Asia to Australia probably arrived over a long period of time, rather than all at once. They were hunter-gatherers, and settled along the coastline and in the valleys of major rivers, where food was probably most plentiful.

Animals in Australia at that time included giant kangaroos and wallabies, and a creature called a diprotodon, which could weigh up to two tonnes. No evidence has yet been found of anything so large being killed and eaten. Eels and shellfish were plentiful, and edible plants included wild millet and a kind of yam.

These early settlers were the first Aborigines (native Australians). They lived in the mouths of caves or in rock shelters, and made their tools and weapons from stone and bone. Many of the stones they needed must have been available on the surface, but on the south coast people mined flint from Koonalda Cave, which is 305 metres long. They also created the earliest known rock art in the world, by carving some swirling patterns on rocks at Panaramittee around 45,000 years ago.

MOVING INLAND

As the ice melted, and sea levels rose, the land bridges were slowly flooded. By 5000 BC, Tasmania was cut off from mainland Australia, which was cut off by a wider stretch of ocean from the rest of the world. Low-lying coastal areas were flooded, too, and people moved farther inland, adapting to the increasing aridity they found.

Many led a nomadic life in pursuit of food, but in areas where there was a reliable source of water, people could be more settled. They lived in round houses made

◆ *Early Australian art included paintings on rock. Some are known as X-ray paintings because they show an animal's bones and internal organs.*

◆ *Fire provided light and heat, and also frightened wild animals away. At night, people and their dogs gathered around the fire. Food was cooked in it, by roasting or baking in clay.*

◆ *The Aborigines used the boomerang when hunting. It was carved from hard wood and shaped so that it would return to the thrower if it failed to strike the prey. The hunters also used long spears to catch their prey.*

Their view was that the world was created by the Ancestors, at a time called the Dreamtime. Once the Ancestors finished creating the world, they went back into the earth, but their spirits remained behind.

Each tribal group had its own sacred places where the Ancestors lived. At certain times of year hundreds of people gathered to celebrate the harvest of foods from the wild. The Aborigines thought that they belonged to the land and not the other way round.

from stone, rather than in temporary shelters. They did not need to start farming, as they could take all they wanted from the wild.

They continued to paint and carve pictures on rocks, some relating to their beliefs.

◆ Smaller kangaroos provided the Aborigines with one of their main sources of meat, but they also ate various grubs and moths, as well as flying foxes and turtle eggs.

Kangaroos

◆ The Aborigines believed that the landscape was created by rainbow serpents as they wriggled inland from the sea. The earliest rock paintings of them date from around 4000 BC, when Gorrodolmi and his wife are said to have painted themselves on a rock at Wirlin-gunyang.

Spear-throwing

◆ Aboriginal hunters used spears to catch some of their prey. The long handles came from smoothed wood and the point was made from hard, sharpened stones, such as flint.

THE PEOPLE OF THE PACIFIC ISLANDS

1800 BC–AD 600

People settled on the smaller islands of the Pacific Ocean over a period of around 3,000 years, from 1800 BC onwards, but the larger islands of Indonesia, New Guinea and western Melanesia were settled earlier, at around the same time as people went to Australia. The people of these islands were largely fishermen and farmers, cultivating banana, yam, taro, sago, coconut and breadfruit, which had originally grown in the wild. They domesticated pigs and chickens for food and perhaps also had dogs as pets.

By 1800 BC shipbuilders in Indonesia were skilled enough to make large canoes, which could be rowed or sailed for long distances. People also knew how to find their way at sea by studying the stars and the patterns of the ocean currents. With this knowledge, families set out to discover new lands.

They took food for the journey, and animals and food plants and seeds, so that they could start farming as soon as they found somewhere suitable. They settled first on the islands of Micronesia, just to the north of the equator.

◆ *Early voyagers to the Polynesian islands probably used two canoes, fixed together with a platform, to carry passengers, animals and plants. They might well have added to their diet on board by fishing with lines over the edge of the canoe as they went along.*

Some of these were probably settled also by people from the Philippines. By 1300 BC people from Indonesia had settled on the most easterly islands of the Melanesian group, too.

The group of islands known as Polynesia is spread over about 20 million square kilometres, 99 percent of which is water. The westernmost islands were settled from around 1500 BC by people from farther east, who are known as Lapita. They made fine pottery, as well as stone tools, and used shells to make ornaments and fish-hooks.

By 1000 BC, the Lapita culture was established as far east as Tonga and Samoa, and

Transplanting

Most of the islands which were settled in this period had similar climates to the lands the migrants had left. Therefore, the plants and animals they took with them soon flourished in their new environment. The four foods shown here are still cultivated on the islands.

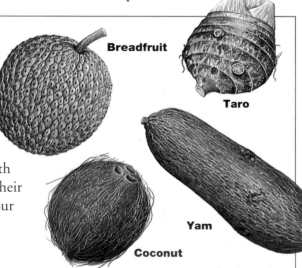

Breadfruit

Taro

Yam

Coconut

from there people set out to look for other islands in the rest of the Polynesian triangle. By 150 BC their descendants had settled on the Society Islands and the Marquesas Islands. By AD 400 they had reached Easter Island, which was the most southeasterly point, and Hawaii, the most northerly point. They did not reach the most southwesterly point of the triangle, New Zealand, until about AD 900.

The people who settled on the islands lived in village communities, and traded goods amongst themselves and with other islanders. Coloured feathers, for instance from the bird of paradise, were especially valued, as they were used to decorate the clothes of important people. People of each island developed their own style of wood and stone carving. The knowledge of metalworking never spread any farther than western New Guinea. So the people of the islands continued making their tools from stone, wood, bone and shell.

From about AD 100, pottery disappears from archaeological sites. This is probably because so many natural containers, such as gourds and coconut shells, were available. Another reason might have been that people changed from boiling their food in pots over the fire, to baking it in underground earth ovens.

◆ The islanders ate the flesh and drank the milk of coconuts, and used the empty shells as containers. They took timber from the trunk of the coconut palm, for the posts of their houses and for bridges, and they thatched roofs with the leaves. The fibres surrounding the coconuts were crushed and twisted, to make ropes and cords.

Typical Polynesian house

◆ Most houses on the Pacific islands were made from a wooden framework, thatched with palm leaves. Some of them were built on stone floors, but in wet areas some were built on a frame above the water.

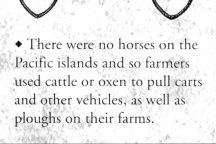

Cattle yoke used by farmers

◆ There were no horses on the Pacific islands and so farmers used cattle or oxen to pull carts and other vehicles, as well as ploughs on their farms.

◆ These pottery fragments were found on the Santa Cruz Islands. They were made by people of the Lapita culture and date from around 1100 BC. They are stamped with a face motif, or pattern.

word of mouth from one generation to the next. Another similarity was that many artefacts were made from organic materials, such as wood, bark and leaves, which rotted away quickly in the warm, wet atmosphere of most of the islands.

These two facts make it difficult to find out many details of the early civilizations on the Pacific Islands, but we do know something of their religion, including the names of some of their gods, such as Tangaroa Upao Vahu who was the chief god of the Polynesians.

◆ The most mysterious archaeological remains in Polynesia are a series of around 1,000 enormous stone statues on Easter Island. They have been carved from a soft volcanic rock and each one weighs around 50 tonnes. They were probably carved at the quarry where the blocks of stone were cut. Then they were transported on a wooden sledge, which was pushed on rollers made from tree trunks to the site where they were erected. Ropes and levers were used to pull them upright.

DIFFERENT ISLANDS, DIFFERENT CULTURES

The islands of the Pacific varied a great deal in size, shape and geography. Some had high mountains and steep cliffs, while others were low-lying with sandy beaches and lagoons. Some, such as Hawaii, even had active volcanoes. These differences in environment affected the way people lived and over the centuries different cultures began to develop.

In spite of this, many similarities also remained. For example, there was no system of writing and so people had to pass on their knowledge by

STONE STATUES

Stone platforms called *marae* have been excavated on some islands and it is thought that religious ceremonies were carried out on them.

The most famous platform is the one on Easter Island which was surrounded by huge statues carved from stone. The statues originally showed figures from the hips up, but many of them have become buried up to the neck, and now show just the heads. They are ancestor figures and are thought to have had some religious importance.

GLOSSARY OF TERMS

EXPLANATION OF UNUSUAL AND SIGNIFICANT WORDS AND
TERMS FOUND IN THIS BOOK

adobe ♦ a building material like a brick made from clay and dried in the sun.

ambassador ♦ an important person, sent by one ruler to visit another on his or her behalf.

artefact ♦ any object which has been made by people.

bard ♦ a Celtic poet and storyteller who often sang as well as recited.

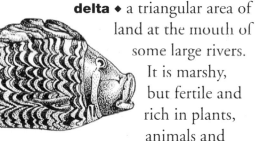

Fish-shaped bottle, an artefact from ancient Egypt

caste system ♦ the system by which Hindu society was organized. It was based on a system used by the Aryans and divided people into different classes, which were decided by birth and could not be changed.

chainmail ♦ body armour made up of many iron rings, linked together like a chain.

civilizations ♦ distinct ways of life, taking in the different kinds of accommodation, writing, political systems and so on, which affect large groups of people at any one time.

chronology ♦ the arrangement of events in the order of the time in which they took place.

delta ♦ a triangular area of land at the mouth of some large rivers. It is marshy, but fertile and rich in plants, animals and birds.

dendrochronology ♦ a method of dating timber, by studying the pattern of the growth rings in it and comparing them with those of another piece of timber of a known date.

digging stick ♦ a pointed stick, used for digging up the ground so that seeds can be planted.

draft animal ♦ an animal that can be used to pull a heavy load such as a wheeled vehicle, a sledge or a plough.

ecofact ♦ a naturally produced object found on an archaeological site, such as the remains of plants and animals.

ecology ♦ the scientific study of how living organisms relate to each other and their environment.

evolution ♦ the gradual process by which living organisms have developed since the start of life.

excavate ♦ to dig up a site in order to reveal anything lying underneath the surface.

flax ♦ a plant with blue flowers. Fibres from its stem can be spun to make linen yarn, which can be woven into cloth.

flint ♦ a smooth, hard rock which was chipped with other rocks to make sharp edges, useful for scraping and cutting.

fossil ♦ the remains of a plant or animal that lived in the past and has been preserved, usually because its organic material has been replaced by minerals.

fresco ♦ a painting done onto freshly laid, wet plaster and left to dry with the plaster. The painting is part of the wall.

game ♦ wild animals, such as birds and fish, which are hunted for food.

geologist ♦ someone who studies rocks and minerals.

gourd ♦ a large fruit. When the flesh has been scraped out, the rind can be dried and used as a waterproof container.

grave goods ♦ any items, such as jewellery, weapons or food, which were buried with the dead to help them on their journey to the next life.

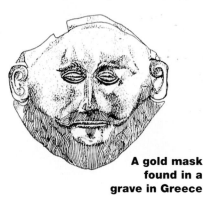

A gold mask found in a grave in Greece

interpret ♦ to explain something, based on evidence.

irrigate ♦ to bring water to growing crops by some artificial method, such as building wells, dams or canals.

labyrinth ♦ a system of underground passages, full of twists and dead ends, making it difficult to find a way through.

mastaba ♦ an early Egyptian tomb with sloping sides and a flat top. It was built over a burial pit to make it stand out.

menhir ♦ a tall upright stone which stands alone. There are many in Brittany and its name is from the Breton *men*, meaning 'stone', and *hir*, meaning 'long'.

metate ♦ a simple grinding device, in which grain is placed on a flat stone and a smaller stone is rubbed back and forth by hand across it.

monsoon wind system ♦ the pattern of winds in the Indian Ocean. In summer they blow from the south west and in winter from the north east.

mosaic ♦ a picture or pattern made up of many tiny pieces of coloured stone or marble.

A tiny mosaic on an earring made in South America

myth ♦ a story from long ago passed on from generation to generation, often used to explain natural or historical events.

nomarch ♦ the ruler of one of the 42 *nomes*, or provinces, of ancient Egypt. He carried out the pharaoh's wishes and took his rule to the people.

obsidian ♦ a dark volcanic rock which looks like thick glass. It can be polished to a sharp edge and used for knife blades. Large pieces can also be polished and used as mirrors.

palisade ♦ a strong fence of pointed wooden stakes set very close together.

papyrus ♦ a reed which grew along the banks of the Nile. The pith from its stem was made into sheets for writing on.

pemmican ♦ meat which was dried in strips to preserve it. It could be cut up and mixed with melted fat to be eaten.

philosophy ♦ the search for wisdom and knowledge.

pictograms ♦ a system of writing which uses symbols based on simple pictures of objects, rather than letters.

post hole ♦ a mark left in the soil, where a post supporting a building or a fence once stood. Although the wood has long since rotted away, the soil which replaces it is usually different from that around it.

press ◆ a device into which grapes or olives are placed and crushed with weights to squeeze out the juice or oil.

radiocarbon dating ◆ a method of dating things which were once alive. During their lifetime, they absorbed carbon, including carbon-14 which is radioactive. When a living organism dies, no more carbon is absorbed and the carbon-14 starts to decay. Scientists know how long this process takes and so by measuring the amount of carbon-14 left in an object, they can tell when it died.

rampart ◆ an earthwork built to defend some sort of site, such as a fort.

reincarnation ◆ the passing of a person's soul into another body after death.

rescue archaeology ◆ excavations that have to be carried out in an especially limited time, usually because the site is needed for some other purpose, such as new construction work.

satrapy ◆ the name given to one of 20 provinces of the Persian empire. Representatives from each had to bring large tributes to the palace at Persepolis.

semi-arid ◆ an area that has a little rainfall, but not enough to allow many trees or crops to grow.

seven wonders of the ancient world ◆ a list made by Greek writers in the 2nd century BC: the Great Pyramid at Giza, the Hanging Gardens of Babylon, the Statue of Zeus at Olympia, the Temple of Diana at Ephesus, the Mausoleum at Halicarnassus, the Colossus of Rhodes and a lighthouse called the Pharos of Alexandria. Only the pyramid survives.

silt ◆ fine particles of soil which are carried along in river water.

steppes ◆ the plains of south-east Europe and parts of Asia.

terracotta ◆ a substance made from clay and sand, which can be hardened in the heat of an oven called a kiln and is used to make pottery. Terracotta was used for pots as well as statues.

thermoluminescence ◆ a method used for dating pottery which has been hardened by firing in a kiln.

toga ◆ a Roman garment, made from one piece of cloth which was draped around the body.

tribute ◆ money or goods that had to be paid at certain times, usually by a conquered people to their conqueror.

trireme ◆ a large Greek wooden ship with three banks of oars one on top of the other on both sides of the boat.

tundra ◆ an almost treeless area next to the polar ice. All but the top few inches of soil are permanently frozen and so only a few plants can grow.

typology ◆ a method of dating objects by comparing them with another object of a similar style and a known date.

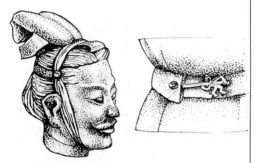

Details from the terracotta army found in Shi Huangdi's tomb in China

wattle and daub ◆ a building material made from interwoven twigs covered in mud or clay.

THE AMERICAS

BC

50-35,000 ◆ First people cross from Asia, using a land bridge caused by the Ice Age.

13,000 ◆ Bluefish Cave, the earliest known site in the Yukon area, is occupied.

11,000 ◆ Monte Verde, a village in southern Chile, thrives.

10,000 ◆ As the ice sheets retreat, more settlements are established.

8000 ◆ The first known burials in North America take place.

7000 ◆ Start of crop cultivation in the Tehuacán Valley in Mexico.

6300 ◆ Potatoes grown in Peru.

5000 ◆ Maize cultivated in Mexico.

5400 ◆ People in Peru start to herd llamas and alpacas.

3500 ◆ First cotton grown in Peru and used to make cloth, twine and fishing-nets.

3372 ◆ First date on the Maya calendar.

2800 ◆ Villages appear in Amazonia. People grow food in small plots like gardens.

1500 ◆ Stone temples are built in Mexico.

1200 ◆ The Olmec civilization develops in Mexico.

Hollow Olmec pottery figure found on the site of Tlatlico, in Mesoamerica

EUROPE

BC

33,000 ◆ Much of northern Europe is covered by ice.

30,000 ◆ Cave art begins in Spain and France.

8300 ◆ The ice retreats. This marks the start of the Mesolithic (or Middle Stone) Age.

5200 ◆ Farming spreads as far as the Netherlands.

5000 ◆ People in the Balkans make copper and gold objects.

3200 ◆ The building of Stonehenge in England begins.

2450 ◆ Skara Brae in the Orkneys is destroyed in a storm.

2300 ◆ Start of the European Bronze Age.

2000 ◆ Minoan Crete dominates the Mediterranean.

Dice from Skara Brae

1650 ◆ Mycenaean culture develops in Greece.

1450 ◆ A volcanic eruption on Thera (now Santorini) causes great damage in the Aegean.

1100 ◆ The Dorians invade Greece from the north and the Greek Dark Ages begin.

800 ◆ Etruscan city-states are established in central Italy. Celtic culture develops north of the Alps.

776 ◆ The first Olympic games take place in Greece.

750 ◆ Ironworking in Britain.

510 ◆ The last king of Rome is deposed and a republic is formed.

450 ◆ Athens reaches the peak of its power.

AFRICA, INCLUDING EGYPT

BC

100,000 ◆ Earliest evidence for modern humans (*Homo sapiens sapiens*) in southern Africa and the Near East.

24,000 ◆ Rock paintings found in Apollo 11 Cave in Namibia are the earliest art dated in Africa.

8500 ◆ Earliest rock art in the Sahara, depicting giraffes, elephants and hippopotamuses.

7500 ◆ First pottery produced in the Sahara.

6500 ◆ Wild cattle are domesticated in the Sahara.

4000 ◆ Sails are used on boats in Egypt.

3100 ◆ Menes unites Upper and Lower Egypt.

2650 ◆ The Step Pyramid is built in Egypt.

2575 ◆ Start of the Old Kingdom in Egypt.

1800 ◆ The horse is introduced into Egypt.

1730 ◆ Hyksos invade Egypt and the Israelites settle there.

1550 ◆ Start of the New Kingdom in Egypt.

1270 ◆ Israelites leave Egypt.

1200 ◆ Rock carvings showing chariots are made in the Sahara, which can still be crossed by traders moving north and south.

1179 ◆ The Sea People attack Egypt.

1163 ◆ Rameses III, the last great pharaoh of Egypt, dies.

1070 ◆ End of the New Kingdom in Egypt.

900 ◆ The kingdom of Kush gains independence.

THE NEAR AND MIDDLE EAST

BC

10,000 ◆ Agriculture starts in the Fertile Crescent.

9000 ◆ Sheep domesticated in northern Mesopotamia.

8000 ◆ Wheat, barley and pulses cultivated in the Fertile Crescent.

7000 ◆ Çatal Hüyük in Anatolia is founded and the first Near Eastern pottery is made.

6500 ◆ Earliest known textiles (linen) woven in Çatal Hüyük.

6200 ◆ Copper is used on a small scale in Çatal Hüyük.

5500 ◆ The earliest known irrigation system is in use in Mesopotamia.

4500 ◆ First sails used on ships.

3760 ◆ Bronze in use.

3100 ◆ The Sumerians invent a system of writing.

3000 ◆ Wheeled vehicles in use.

2360 ◆ The city-states of southern Mesopotamia are united under Sargon of Akkad.

2100 ◆ Abraham and his family leave Ur to go to Canaan.

1700 ◆ Bronze armour worn.

1650 ◆ Foundation of the Hittite kingdom.

1595 ◆ Hittites conquer Babylon.

1300 ◆ Medes and Persians move into Iran.

1116 ◆ Assyrians conquer Babylon.

1000 ◆ Phoenicians become the main trading power in the Levant.

922 ◆ Israel splits into Israel and Judah.

650 ◆ The first coins are used in Lydia in Anatolia.

INDIA AND THE FAR EAST

BC

16,000 ◆ The earliest known pottery in the world is made in Japan.

9000 ◆ Pottery in use in China.

6500 ◆ Farming develops in India.

6000 ◆ Farming villages are established in China.

5000 ◆ Wet rice farming starts in China.

4000 ◆ Jade is imported to China from 3000 kilometres away to make ornaments and weapons.

3500 ◆ Copper is used in Thailand.

3000 ◆ First evidence of agriculture in Korea where millet is grown.

2700 ◆ Silk weaving and bronzeworking flourish in China.

2500 ◆ Towns develop in the Indus Valley. The oldest known woven cotton cloth is made in Mohenjo-Daro.

Beads from Mohenjo-Daro

2200 ◆ Late Jomon culture thriving in Japan.

1500 ◆ Aryans begin their invasion of the Indus Valley.

1000 ◆ The Chinese introduce bronzeworking into Korea.

800 ◆ City-states, supported by rice farming, develop in the Ganges Valley in India.

600 ◆ War elephants are used in battles in India.

563 ◆ The birth of the Buddha in India.

551 ◆ The birth of the Chinese philosopher Confucius.

OCEANIA

BC

53,000 ◆ The first people reach Australia, taking advantage of the narrow seas and land-bridges which result from the Ice Age.

45,000 ◆ Earliest known rock art in the world, found in South Australia.

25,000 ◆ Settlement expands to include New Guinea, the southeast coast of Australia and Tasmania.

8000 ◆ Sea levels start to rise again after the Ice Age.

7000 ◆ Agriculture begins in New Guinea, based on root crops.

5000 ◆ As sea levels rise farther, coastal settlements in Australia are flooded and Tasmania becomes an island.

4000 ◆ Colonization of the Pacific islands begins.

1500 ◆ The dingo is introduced to Australia.

1500 ◆ The Lapita people start to expand from their homeland in Indonesia towards Melanesia and western Polynesia.

1000 ◆ Lapita culure is established on the islands of Fiji, Tonga and Samoa.

1000 ◆ In Australia long-distance networks are set up for the exchange and trade of ornaments and raw materials. In the southeast of the country there are large villages of round stone-built houses.

THE AMERICAS

1200 ◆ The Chavin culture appears in Peru.
1000 ◆ Start of the Adena culture in the eastern woodlands of North America.
310 ◆ Beginning of the Hopewell culture in the eastern woodlands of North America.
300 ◆ Rise of Maya civilization in Mesoamerica.
200 ◆ Rise of Nazca civilization on the southern Peruvian coast.

AD
1 ◆ Moche civilization dominates the coast of northern Peru. The Basketmaking culture develops in the south west of North America and another complex culture develops on the Pacific coast.
50 ◆ Teotihuacán starts to be built as a planned city in Mesoamerica.
200 ◆ The Hopewell people build huge burial mounds in Ohio.
400 ◆ The Incas establish their first settlements in Peru. The Marajoara culture starts on Marajo Island in the mouth of the Amazon River.
500 ◆ In Mesoamerica Teotihuacán reaches the height of its power. In South America the central and southern Andes are dominated by the Tiahuanaco and Huari empires.

EUROPE

431 ◆ Start of the Peloponnesian War between Athens and Sparta.
390 ◆ The Celts sack Rome.
336 ◆ Alexander the Great comes to power.
300 ◆ Rome gains power in Italy.
264 ◆ Start of the Punic Wars between Rome and Carthage.
206 ◆ Rome controls Spain.
49 ◆ Julius Caesar rules Rome until 44.
27 ◆ Octavian becomes the first Roman emperor.

Octavian

AD
43 ◆ The Romans invade Britain.
79 ◆ The Roman towns of Pompeii and Herculaneum are buried by an eruption of Mount Vesuvius.
117 ◆ The Roman empire reaches its greatest extent.
126 ◆ In Britain, Hadrian's Wall is completed.
286 ◆ The Roman empire is divided into two.
330 ◆ Constantine makes Constantinople the capital of the Roman empire.
370 ◆ Huns invade Europe.
410 ◆ Rome is sacked by Visigoths. The Western Empire collapses.
452 ◆ Attila the Hun enters Italy.
527 ◆ Justinian becomes the Byzantine emperor and tries to revive the old Roman empire.

AFRICA, INCLUDING EGYPT

750 ◆ The king of Kush conquers Egypt. Earliest evidence for the Phoenician settlement at Carthage.
600 ◆ The Nubian capital moves to Meroë as ironworking becomes more important.
500 ◆ Darius I completes a canal to connect the Nile and the Red Sea.
400 ◆ Earliest known ironworking south of the Sahara is on the Jos Plateau in Nigeria.
400 ◆ Nok culture flourishes in west Africa.
332 ◆ Alexander the Great conquers Egypt.
323 ◆ Ptolemy I rules Egypt.
146 ◆ The Romans destroy Carthage.
100 ◆ Camels are introduced to the Sahara.
30 ◆ Egypt becomes a Roman province.

AD
1 ◆ Bantu people begin to migrate to east Africa.
50 ◆ The kingdom of Axum in Ethiopia begins to expand.
350 ◆ Axum conquers the kingdom of Kush. Christianity reaches Ethiopia.
400 ◆ Jenne-jeno, the first town south of the Sahara, is established.
429 ◆ The Vandals start to overrun the Roman empire in north Africa and set up their own kingdom there.
500 ◆ Bantu people reach southern Africa, bringing with them domesticated cattle and the knowledge of ironworking.

THE NEAR AND MIDDLE EAST

609 ◆ End of the Assyrian empire.
550 ◆ Around the Red Sea and the Gulf of Aden new states develop, based on the overland trade in frankincense and myrrh from southern Arabia to the eastern Mediterranean.
525 ◆ Persia conquers Egypt.
499 ◆ The Persian empire is at its height.
334 ◆ Alexander the Great begins his conquest of Persia.
312 ◆ Seleucids control Syria.
240 ◆ Start of the Parthian dynasty in northern Persia.
53 ◆ Parthians prevent Romans expanding empire farther east.
5 ◆ The birth of Jesus.

AD

1 ◆ Discovery of the monsoon wind system increases trade between the Red Sea and the Indian Ocean.
30 ◆ Jesus is crucified.
70 ◆ Romans destroy Jerusalem. The Diaspora (or dispersal) of the Jews begins.
224 ◆ Sassanians start to rule the Persian empire.
300 ◆ Maritime trade replaces the overland trade in incense and spices, and the south Arabian kingdoms start to decline.
330 ◆ Constantinople becomes capital of the Roman empire.
484 ◆ The Huns attack Persia and kill the emperor.
529 ◆ The emperor Justinian sets out to conquer the Near East.
579 ◆ The Sassanian empire of Persia reaches its greatest extent.

INDIA AND THE FAR EAST

550 ◆ The first important production of iron in China.
400 ◆ Ironworking is introduced to Korea.
300 ◆ Wet rice agriculture is practised in Japan.
322 ◆ The Mauryan dynasty comes to power in northern India.
273 ◆ Start of the rule of Asoka in India. He introduces Buddhism to his people.
250 ◆ Buddhism in Sri Lanka.
221 ◆ Qin dynasty in China.
218 ◆ Work to complete the Great Wall of China begins.
202 ◆ Han dynasty in China.
108 ◆ China controls Korea.
100 ◆ Buddhism spreads east from India along the trade routes.
50 ◆ Chinese silk is traded with the Romans.

AD

105 ◆ Paper invented in China.
200 ◆ The Yamato start to dominate Japan.
220 ◆ Start of a period of civil war in China which lasts until 589.
320 ◆ The Gupta dynasty comes to power in northern India.
360 ◆ The Japanese start to conquer Korea.
400 ◆ Buddhist cave-temples are built along the Silk Road.
475 ◆ Wall paintings are done in the Buddhist cave-temples at Ajanta in India.
535 ◆ In India the Gupta empire collapses.
594 ◆ Buddhism becomes the official religion of Japan.
618 ◆ The Tang dynasty comes to power in China.

OCEANIA

150 ◆ The Marquesas Islands are colonized by Lapita settlers.

AD

200 ◆ The Lapita civilization disappears in the western Pacific, along with pottery-making skills.
300 ◆ The first settlers arrive in Tahiti.
400 ◆ Polynesian settlers reach Easter Island and the Hawaiian Islands.

A typical Polynesian hut

GLOSSARY OF PEOPLE AND PLACES

FURTHER DETAILS ON INDIVIDUALS, NATIONS AND LANDS

Akkad ◆ also known as Agade, this city was founded by King Sargon after he took over the throne of Kish on the Euphrates River. Akkad was nearby, but its location is not yet known.

Anatolia ◆ another name for Asia Minor, the part of Asia which had the Black Sea to the north, the Aegean Sea to the west and the Mediterranean to the south.

Angles ◆ people from Schleswig, an area in modern-day Denmark, who migrated to eastern Britain. East Anglia is called after them, as is England itself.

Aramaic ◆ the language of Syria which was widely used in the Middle East at the time of Jesus. Its name comes from Aramaios, the Greek name for Syria.

Aristotle ◆ a Greek philosopher and scientist. He was at one time tutor to Alexander the Great and with his assistance founded a research community in Athens called the Lyceum. He died in 322 BC.

Assur ◆ also known as Ashur, this was the ancient capital of Assyria. It was a great trading centre and remained the religious capital and burial place of the kings even after the government moved to Nineveh.

Attila ◆ born around AD 406, he became king of the Huns with his brother Bleda in 434. Eleven years later, he killed Bleda. In 447 he marched on Constantinople and was paid to leave. Four years later he invaded Gaul but was defeated. He then attacked Italy, but eventually had to withdraw and in 453 he died.

Brahma ◆ the creator god of the Hindu religion. He is often shown with four heads and four arms.

Burgundians ◆ one of the Scandinavian tribes which moved south after the fall of the Roman empire and gave its name to the Burgundy area of France.

Bushmen ◆ hunters and gatherers, a few of whom still follow their traditional way of life in parts of Botswana. Their rock paintings can be found in many parts of South Africa.

Byzantium ◆ the ancient name for Istanbul. It was renamed Constantinople in AD 324 by the emperor Constantine when it became capital of the Roman empire. When the power of Rome collapsed, this was renamed the Byzantine empire.

Alexander the Great, pupil of Aristotle

Dorians ◆ people who invaded Greece from the north around 1100 BC. They spoke a form of Greek and kept Mycenaean legends alive in long poems. They also introduced the use of iron for swords.

Elam ◆ a kingdom in southwest Iran. Its capital was at Susa and it had a holy city at Dur-Untash with a ziggurat six storeys high.

Euclid ◆ a Greek mathematician who lived around 300 BC. He is famous for his work on geometry.

Franks ◆ a Germanic tribe which migrated south after the fall of the Roman empire. They defeated the Burgundians and settled in what had been Gaul, which was then named France after them.

Gaul ◆ the Roman name for France and for the Celts who lived there.

Goths ◆ a Germanic tribe which possibly moved south from Scandinavia. In the 3rd century AD, they split into two groups – the Ostrogoths and the Visigoths.

Hallstatt ◆ an early Celtic site in the Austrian Alps. Its people grew wealthy from mining and trading salt. Many artefacts were recovered from there in the 19th century when around 1,000 graves were excavated. The first phase of Celtic civilization is named after this site.

Hannibal ◆ the Carthaginian general who is famous for taking 50,000 soldiers and 38 war elephants across the Alps in 15 days to attack the Romans. He won three important victories against them between 218 and 216 BC. The Romans fought back by sending their general Scipio to attack Carthage. Hannibal returned to Africa and was defeated in 202 BC.

Hattushash ◆ the capital of the Hittites. It was defended by stone walls of great strength. In the 1930s, over 3,000 cuneiform tablets were found here.

Hippocrates ◆ a Greek doctor, born in the 5th century BC. He travelled widely in Greece and Asia Minor. The Hippocratic oath that medical students take today is named after him.

Greek relief sculpture of a doctor

hominids ◆ modern humans and their human-like ancestors. The latter are split into four groups: *Australopithecus*, *Homo habilis*, *Homo erectus* and *Home sapiens*.

Huns ◆ a nomadic people whose original home was in Mongolia. They were expert horse riders and skilled fighters. They were united under Attila, but after his death their importance declined.

Hyksos ◆ a nomadic tribe from Asia who moved south through Palestine and Syria to invade the delta area of Egypt.

Judas Maccabeus ◆ a Jewish leader who led the rebellion against Antiochus IV's persecution of the Jews in Judah in 167 BC, after Antiochus dedicated the Temple in Jerusalem to the worship of the Greek god, Zeus. In 164 BC Jewish worship was restored.

Julius Caesar ◆ a Roman aristocrat and soldier who was born around 100 BC. By 60 BC he had been elected consul and decided which provinces he wanted to govern. In the next ten years he conquered vast new territories for Rome, including Gaul, but he failed to conquer Britain. He schemed until he was made sole ruler of Rome for life, but in 44 BC he was killed by two senators who thought he wanted to make himself king and abolish the republic.

Larsa ◆ a city-state with a palace on the Euphrates River between Ur and Babylon. When Larsa was at its height, its king ruled over ten or so less important kings.

La Tène ◆ a Celtic site on Lake Neuchâtel in Switzerland. It is now under water, but it was an important farming and trading settlement dating from around 500 BC. Artefacts found there are different in style from those found at Hallstatt, and La Tène has given its name to the later Celtic period.

Marathon ◆ a battle on the east coast of Greece in 490 BC, in which a small force of Athenians defeated the Persians. It gave its name to the marathon race because the Athenian runner Pheidippides ran about 42 kilometres (the same distance as a modern marathon) from the battlefield to Athens with news of the victory.

Mari ◆ a city and a kingdom in Mesopotamia. It stood on the Euphrates River at a point where three trade routes met. Tin, copper, silver, lapis lazuli, timber and textiles were traded there.

Medes ◆ a semi-nomadic tribe from Media, a region to the south west of the Caspian Sea. They migrated to Iran at the same time as the Persians and at first were the more powerful of the two peoples.

Moses ◆ the lawgiver of Israel who led his people out of slavery in Egypt. According to the Old Testament, the journey back to Israel, which was also called the Promised Land, took 40 years. It is said Moses died aged 120.

Napata ◆ the original capital of the kingdom of Kush. As iron-working became important, the capital moved upstream to Meroë where iron ore was plentiful.

Ostrogoths ◆ one of the two distinct groups of Goths, split during the 3rd century AD. The name means 'the eastern Goths'. They settled in the south east of Europe, but lost their lands to the Huns in AD 370.

Paul (Saint) ◆ one of the followers of Jesus who spread Christianity throughout the eastern Mediterranean from AD 45 onwards. His 13 Epistles, or letters, are a large part of the New Testament. In AD 67 he was executed in Rome.

Peloponnesian War ◆ a war between Athens and Sparta which started in 431 BC and lasted until 404 BC. The Spartans under Lysander were victorious.

Philistines ◆ a warlike, seafaring people who settled in Canaan after being forced out of Egypt. They strongly resisted the Israelites when they in turn returned from Egypt. The part of Canaan where they lived was named Palestine.

Philistine burial jar

Phrygians ◆ people from Thrace who settled in a part of Anatolia called Phrygia after the fall of the Hittites. Their capital was at Gordium and they are said to have invented embroidery.

Plato ◆ a Greek philosopher, born in Athens in 429 BC. He was one of Socrates' students and lived to be over 70 years old.

Pythagoras ◆ a Greek philosopher and mathematician who died in 497 BC.

Salamis ◆ the site of a naval battle in 480 BC between the Greeks and the Persians. The Greeks in their triremes drove the Persian ships into a confused huddle and defeated them.

Saxons ◆ one of the Germanic tribes which migrated to south and east Britain after the Romans left.

Scythians ◆ a nomadic people who lived north of the Black Sea from the 6th century BC. They traded with the Greeks and were skilled artists and metalworkers.

Seleucids ◆ the ruling dynasty in the eastern part of Alexander the Great's empire after Alexander's death. It was founded by Seleucus I Nicator who had been one of Alexander's generals.

Socrates ◆ the most famous of the Greek philosophers. He was born in Athens in 469 BC. His protests against tyranny led to his trial and in 399 BC he was condemned to death.

Telamon ◆ a battle which took place in 225 BC between the Romans and the Celts after around 70,000 Celts from various tribes united to attack Rome. On their way back to their homelands, they were trapped between two Roman armies which were superior in skill. The Celts fought bravely, but around 40,000 of them were killed and 10,000 taken prisoner.

Thermopylae ◆ a land battle in 480 BC during the Greek-Persian wars. The Persians won, but the Spartan king, Leonidas, and 300 men defended the pass at Thermopylae for three days to allow the rest of the Greek army to escape. Their heroism inspired the Greeks to continue the war and in the following year they defeated the Persians.

Thrace ◆ a region in the north of the Balkans which was famous for its horses and its horsemen. Its coasts were colonized by the Greeks in the 8th century BC, but later it was invaded by the Persians, the Macedonians and the Romans.

Trojan War ◆ a legendary war, described in Homer's *Iliad*. It was caused when Paris, son of the king of Troy, eloped with Helen, wife of Menelaus, king of Sparta. Menelaus's brother, Agamemnon, king of Mycenae, raised an army and besieged Troy. Excavations at Troy show that the city was involved in a war at a time which fits in with the legend.

Uruk ◆ one of the earliest Sumerian cities and a religious centre. Pottery dating from around 5000 BC has been found there. Its rulers tried to lead Sumer until Ur became more powerful, but Uruk still remained important as a holy city.

Vandals ◆ a Germanic people who migrated south from Scandinavia, through Europe to Spain and north Africa where they set up a kingdom in AD 429. In AD 455 they sacked Rome and caused so much damage that the modern term vandalism comes from their name.

Vedas ◆ the sacred books of the Hindus which were written in Sanskrit, the language spoken in northwest India from around 1500 BC. The Vedas are divided into four main books, each of which contains hymns, prayers, details of spells and rituals.

Vishnu ◆ an important Hindu god who is known as the Preserver. He appears in ten different forms. The most famous are Rama and Krishna.

Visigoths ◆ the western branch of the Goths, they moved south from the Balkans to attack Rome, and then went on to rule in Gaul and Spain. Their rule in Gaul was brought to an end by the Franks in AD 507, but they ruled in Spain until AD 711.

Zarathustra ◆ also known as Zoroaster, he was an Iranian prophet who was born around 628 BC. He may have been a priest in the old religion of the country which had many different gods when he had a vision of the god Ahura Mazda. He then began preaching a new religion, based on the worship of Ahura Mazda, and most of his teachings are in a book called the *Avesta*, which is the sacred book of Zoroastrianism.

A relief sculpture of a Zoroastrian fire temple

INDEX

Words in **bold** indicate chapters or sections; page numbers in **bold** indicate the same, or glossary entries; page numbers in *italics* indicate illustrations.

The publishers wish to thank the following illustrators
for their contribution to this book:

Jonathan Adams 107*t*; Marion Appleton 37, 128, 129*t*; Norman Bancroft-Hunt 99, 132–3;
Sue Barclay 34; Richard Bonson 142; Vanessa Card all borders and 31*b*, 59*b*, 73*b*, 100*m*, 118;
Stephen Conlin 20*b*, 45*t*; Peter Dennis 14, 22–3, 48, 108–9; Angelika Elsebach 130;
Eugene Fleury maps on 75 and 98; Chris Forsey 23*b*, 45*m*, 121*t*, 129*ml*, 132; Sian Frances 84*b*;
Terry Gabbey 6*b*, 27, 87*t*, 93, 110, 119, 131; Luigi Galante 26, 60*b*; Nicholas Hewetson 21,
41*t*, 65*b*; Adam Hook 66–7, 79*t*, 136*bl*, 136–7*t*; Simon Huson 136*br*; Tony Jackson 129*b*;
Ruth Lindsay 19*b*, 58*b*; Kevin Lyles 81*t*, 112–13*b*; Kevin Maddison 36*t*, 47*t*, 90*t*, 94*m*,
112*tr and bl*, 132; Angus McBride 20*t*, 24–5, 31*t*, 35, 40–1*b*, 44, 50*t*, 83*b*, 90–1*b*, 100–1*b*,
104–5, 120–1*b*; Chris D Orr 15, 126; Nicki Palin 46, 50–1*b*, 51*t*, 61; Jayne Pickering 78*t*;
Malcolm Porter 10*tl*; Eric Robson 56, 58–9*t*, 80, 86, 116–17, 126–7*t*; Bernard Robinson
142–3*t*; Martin Sanders all chapter maps; Rob Shone 8*r*, 60*t*; Mark Stacey 42–3*b*, 74, 96, 111;
Eric Thomas 36–7, 68; George Thompson 42*t*, 65*t*, 107*b*, 144*t*; Gill Tomblin 64, 73*t*, 78–9*b*;
Wendy Webb 18; Andrew Wheatcroft 12, 13, 30, 32, 92, 94–5*b*, 122, 134, 140–1;

and
Jonathan Adams, Karin Ambrose, David Anstey, Tim Bailey, Angelika Elsebach, Chris Forsey,
Terry Gabbey, Allan Hardcastle, Chris Lenthall, Kevin Maddison and Rodney Shackell
for the black and white illustrations.

The publishers also wish to thank the following
for supplying photographs for this book:

4 CM Dixons (CMD); 6 National Museum of Denmark; 7*tl* Werner Formans Archive (WFA);
7*br* The Trustees of the British Museum (BM); 8*tl* Ancient Art and Architecture (AAA);
8*bl* ZEFA; 9*t* Réunion des Musées Nationaux; 9*mr* Mary Evans; 9*bl* Aerofilms; 12 ZEFA;
15, 21, 22 Michael Holford (MH); 27 WFA; 33 MH; 34–5 ZEFA; 36 BM; 40 MH;
49, 55*t* ZEFA; 55*b* Directorate of Archaeology and Museums, Government of Pakistan;
57*t* ZEFA; 57*b* MH; 69 Robert Harding Picture Library (RH); 75 ZEFA; 78 AAA;
82 CM Dixons; 87 ZEFA; 90 MH; 95 WFA; 97 G Dagli Orti; 98, 101, 104, 105 ZEFA;
106 WFA; 109*tl* BM; 109*br* AAA; 110–11 ZEFA; 116 The Hutchison Library;
118 ET Archive; 120 RH; 123*tl* WFA; 123*br* Camerapix; 128–9 Ohio Historical Society;
132 WFA; 135 MH; 137 South American Pictures; 140 WFA.